THE
LOCAL
ADVANTAGE

WHY REAL ESTATE AGENTS ARE CHOOSING
INDEPENDENT OVER BIG BOX BROKERAGES

THE LOCAL ADVANTAGE

WHY REAL ESTATE AGENTS ARE CHOOSING
INDEPENDENT OVER BIG BOX BROKERAGES

JOSH SHIVES

Niche Press
Indianapolis, IN

THE LOCAL ADVANTAGE

Why Real Estate Agents Are Choosing Independent Over Big Box Brokerages

Copyright © 2026 by Josh Shives

All rights reserved. No part of this book may be used or reproduced in any manner whatsoever without prior written consent of the author, except as provided by the United States of America copyright law.

The views, thoughts, and opinions expressed in this publication are solely those of the author, Josh Shives, and do not necessarily reflect the views or positions of any trade organizations, associations, brokerages, or businesses with which he is affiliated. All information is provided for general educational and informational purposes only and should not be construed as legal, financial, or professional advice.

For permission to reprint portions of this content or bulk purchases, contact book@joshshives.com

Author Photograph by: Abby Carlyle at Beyond The Pines Photography

Published by Niche Pressworks; NichePress.com
Indianapolis, IN

ISBN
Hardcover: 978-1-970329-08-7
Paperback: 978-1-970329-09-4
eBook: 978-1-970329-28-5

Library of Congress Cataloging-in-Publication Data on File at lccn.loc.gov

The views expressed herein are solely those of the author and do not necessarily reflect the views of the publisher.

To every agent with a true heart for learning, growing, and making a genuine difference in their community; those who know there's more to real estate than logos and leaderboards; and those who feel the quiet pull toward something better, something local, and something real. This book is for you!

AUTHOR'S NOTE

The insights and stories in this book come from the wins, the misses, and the lessons I've learned while building a locally owned brokerage from the ground up. The lessons I share reflect my personal views and the path that worked for me and my team and don't necessarily represent the official positions or opinions of any real estate associations, trade organizations, or companies I've been part of along the way.

My goal isn't to tell you what to think or where to hang your license. It's to share what I've seen firsthand: that local, independent brokerages can offer a real, values-driven alternative to the Big Box corporate model. There are genuinely good people at almost every company I've ever interacted with, but I hope the ideas shared in *The Local Advantage* help you see new possibilities for your own career, community, and for regaining a sense of purpose in this industry.

The Local Advantage is my story and perspective, offered in the spirit of transparency and encouragement. Take what resonates, leave what doesn't, and build the version of success that fits you best. No matter what you choose, I truly wish you the best and will always be rooting for you.

CONTENTS

CHAPTER 1	Concrete Walls, Open Doors	1
CHAPTER 2	What Real Success Looks Like	9
CHAPTER 3	The St. Elmo Difference	17
CHAPTER 4	The Cost of Comfort	27
CHAPTER 5	The Five Pillars That Change Everything	37
CHAPTER 6	The Real Estate Reality Check	51
CHAPTER 7	When Doubt Gets Loud	61
CHAPTER 8	Time, Money, and Life	75
CHAPTER 9	Why Local and Nimble Wins	89
CHAPTER 10	What Really Matters	99
CHAPTER 11	Claiming Your Local Advantage	107

A Personal Note from Josh	115
Acknowledgements	117
About the Author	119

CHAPTER 1

CONCRETE WALLS, OPEN DOORS

*"Be good to your community, and
your community will be good to you."*

The hum of fluorescent lights was the only sound in the conference room. Our office was inside what used to be a newspaper factory — the bare cinderblock walls and lack of windows made the air so still it felt heavy. The chair legs scraped against the concrete as I took a seat across the conference table from Cheryl, my managing broker. Taking a deep breath, I quickly rubbed my sweaty hands against my slacks before sliding a folded letter across the table.

The old newspaper factory was a space our brokerage's new ownership had chosen when the franchise changed hands. Was it newer? Yes. But brighter? Ehh, I wasn't so sure. The space felt nothing like the old office we'd loved under the previous owner's care. The old place had warmth, personality, and laughter that spilled from one office to another. This new one? It was quiet, sterile, and efficient. A building built for numbers, not people.

"I've made my decision," I said. "I'm leaving."

Cheryl leaned back slightly, eyes soft. "I had a feeling this was coming," she said. "I'm proud of you, Josh. You're going to do great things."

We talked for a few minutes about how I felt the culture had changed and how disconnected things felt since the transition to new ownership. Cheryl really listened the way she always did. She cared. Then she wished me well and promised to send my resignation letter up the chain.

And she did. But the conversation never went further than that conference room. No call from ownership. No "What could we have done differently?" Not even a polite email.

Cheryl didn't own the franchise, and she wasn't part of the corporate ladder. She was just filling a seat so ownership didn't have to show up. My decision to leave stopped exactly where the human connection stopped: with her.

Ten minutes after my conversation with Cheryl, I stepped out of that concrete building and into the sunlight filling the parking lot, blinking against the brightness, realizing that silence can tell you more about a company than any mission statement ever will.

We'd been the number one team at our Big Box brokerage. Listings moved, closings stacked up, and the scoreboard said we were winning. But beneath the spreadsheets and monthly reports, I felt the disconnect growing. Decisions came from people an hour — or a few states — away, people who didn't really know me or our community. The new ownership made it clear that we were a corporate operation now.

I'd known real camaraderie before. The previous franchise owner, Sherrie Cocanower, made the brokerage feel like family. Every first Wednesday of the month, she hosted a Wine Wednesday event where everyone at the office could swap stories, share advice, and actually laugh together. There was warmth in those walls. When ownership changed, the heart of the brokerage left with her. What remained was a slicker version of the business that felt hollow.

On paper, I was doing fine. But something in me was restless. I wanted to work for a company that believed in the same things I did: community, generosity, and connection. I wanted to know the people I worked with and feel the difference our dollars made locally. Instead, we were sending about $60,000 a year up the chain to a corporate office five states away, hoping it somehow came back in value. It felt like throwing a coin into a wishing well and watching it disappear into the water as I crossed my fingers and hoped to someday get what I'd wished for.

The moment I knew my current Big Box brokerage was no longer the place for me came during a conversation about rebranding with my team lead at the time, Christine Clugh-Thomas. She'd been generous, even offering to help transition the team to me someday. Christine was trying to make sure I was set up to succeed, but when we started comparing the money that went out versus what came back, the math didn't make sense. In that moment, I thought, *There has to be a better way than paying for a logo on my shirt.*

> There has to be a better way than paying for a logo on my shirt.

WORDS LIKE A COMPASS

Around that same time, I heard Charlie Shook speak at a charity event in Purdue's Memorial Union Ballroom. If you've never been there, picture high ceilings, polished wood, and a room that smells faintly of old books and history. Charlie was a respected broker in town — technically a competitor, but the kind of competitor you'd still root for — and the keynote speaker that night.

During his presentation, he said one line that stuck in me like an anchor: "Be good to your community, and your community will be good to you."

Simple. Honest. True. It landed hard.

That sentence became my compass, and I started imagining what a brokerage built on that principle might look like — one where decisions were made locally, money stayed in the community, and people genuinely cared about one another. I didn't have the details, but I knew the direction.

THE FIRST BELIEVERS

At home, my wife Cassie and I were our own kind of team — equal parts partnership and friction. I'm the "If there's a will, there's a way" type and Cassie wants the full plan laid out before we move. I'm the dreamer. She's the realist. Together, we make things work.

When I first told her I wanted to start an independent brokerage, she didn't jump for joy. "What's the budget for an office?" she asked. "How much are you spending on staff? What happens if it doesn't work?"

We'd been through a failed business before — one that had nothing to do with real estate but everything to do with heartache. Her questions weren't resistance; they were protection. Still, I couldn't shake the conviction that opening an independent, local brokerage was the right move.

So we made a decision: no rebranding under a franchise. No more sending quarters into the wishing well. Instead, we would build something local, real, and rooted in community.

At first, the goal was a fuzzy someday. Then it sharpened into something we could see.

Ten agents.

Thirty million in closed volume.

Three years to make it happen.

On December 1, 2017, I opened Raeco Realty.

The first month, it was just me laying track — MLS access, transaction systems, software setups, and everything that had to run quietly behind the scenes. We chose the name Raeco as a private nod to our oldest daughter, Raelynn. A blend of "Rae" and "Co.," we wanted a name that meant nothing until we gave it meaning.

In January, two agents joined: Grant Thompson and, soon after, Christine Clugh-Thomas herself. Together, we agreed on a few simple things:

1. We'd show up for the people who live in the communities we serve.
2. We'd use our resources for real systems and local support, not corporate fees.
3. We'd make Raeco a name that stood for professionalism, responsiveness, and respect.

From the outside, it might've looked like we knew exactly what we were doing. But anyone who's ever started a business knows it's part build, part chaos. I made mistakes. Bought expensive software we didn't need. Spent money on a fancy website that was outdated in months. But every wrong turn taught us something.

And we kept going.

Recruiting, though, was humbling. I thought agents would sprint toward higher take-home pay. They didn't. Comfort is powerful. People stay where they feel safe — even if safe means capped income or slow growth. When I'd invite agents to join our brokerage, I'd hear, "Not yet. Maybe after I reach my cap."

Skepticism is fair. I was asking them to trust a brand-new company with no track record. So I focused on two things:

- **First, make the transition easy.** When one agent called late at night and said, "I'm in — and I have a new listing going live tomorrow," I didn't sleep. By sunrise, our local sign vendor, Chris Long, had the post and panel ready. The listing went live that afternoon. From the outside, it looked seamless, and my sleepless night meant it was easy for the agent to transition their work to our company.
- **Second, own our misses and improve.** When we onboarded an agent and forgot to add her to the website for an entire month, that was on me. After that incident, my wife Cassie took over the onboarding process and built a system that worked and included checklists, assets, signatures — everything. When someone said they were ready to join, we could say, "Great, let's go," and mean it.

PROOF AND IGNITION

One Saturday morning about a year after we'd opened Raeco, Cassie was sitting in bed with her laptop open, sunlight streaking across the screen. I was sitting on the other side of the bed and Raelynn was curled up between us. Suddenly, Cassie looked over the top of her computer and said, "Do you see this?"

I leaned around her laptop, squinting at the spreadsheet. The little rectangle she'd highlighted said we'd reached 30 million in closed volume.

I blinked. Looked again. No mistake. No typo. We'd done it.

There was no confetti. No champagne. Just quiet disbelief and a knowing smile between us. For Cassie, it was proof. For me, it was ignition.

Since then, we've kept the same simple philosophy: **Be local on purpose**.

We opened our first office in Lafayette, Indiana, in 2017. Delphi followed in 2022. Monticello in 2025. We allowed growth to happen when it felt right and when the people and values aligned. Because while skill matters, values matter more.

People often ask why I didn't stick with a national brand. My answer's simple: Local matters.

When decisions are made by people who live where you live, the results show up where you can actually see them — on the field, at the fundraiser, in the coffee shop line. Every sponsorship, every hire, every system we choose is built for *here*.

The tools required to start and run a brokerage are out there for everyone now. The real differentiator isn't tech; it's culture. It's whether the logo on your contract means something in your market. Whether you can look your community in the eye and say, "We're here for you," and back it up.

We still have hiccups. Every company does. But we know who we are. We know why we're working this way.

If you're reading this and you feel unseen — successful on paper but disconnected in spirit — there's another path. A path that leads back to the community you serve, and to a company that aligns with your values instead of burying them under bureaucracy.

This book will show you that the corporate model isn't your only option, and that independence doesn't mean isolation. If you've ever felt like a number on a spreadsheet, this is your roadmap to a better way.

In *The Local Advantage,* you'll discover:

- How dramatically different brokerages really are.
- What opportunities you're missing where you are now.
- How to make a smooth, confident transition into a local-first, values-driven model that actually fits your life.

By the end, you'll see what I saw in that conference room years ago: You're not stuck. You're standing at an open door.

Welcome to *The Local Advantage.*

CHAPTER 2

WHAT REAL SUCCESS LOOKS LIKE

"I had to give real estate full gas."

Raeco was established in a small, ground-floor office on 2nd Street in downtown Lafayette, Indiana, just one block from the courthouse. The building was built by John Purdue himself in 1845, and you could feel every year of its history in the walls. Exposed red brick. Heavy stained wood. The kind of craftsmanship that carried the sound of footsteps and stories.

Outside, cars buzzed over old pavement. The windows — tall, original panes with just enough imperfection to bend the light — sent fractured beams of sunlight across the floor and my desk. The air had that quiet mix of age and purpose, like the building itself approved of new ideas as long as you treated it with respect.

That's where I sat the day I left Becky Gibson a voicemail. I told her who I was, what we were building at Raeco Realty, and that I'd love to connect and talk whenever she had a moment. I'd heard great things about her work ethic and how she treated clients, and I could tell she'd fit what we were trying to build.

A few hours later, I was driving home with the windows down to let in the cool, spring afternoon air, one hand on the wheel, the road humming underneath me, when my phone lit up with Becky's name. I thumbed the answer button.

"Hey Becky, Josh Shives with Raeco Realty, we've started a new company and..."

"I appreciate the call, Josh, but I'm happy where I am. No, thank you."

Click.

The wind filled the cab. I glanced at the screen — empty, silent — then back to the road. I respected the directness. She'd already made up her mind, but she still called me back. I made a mental note and kept driving. Raeco was only a few months old, and I was used to being told no.

A few weeks later, in May 2018, Becky agreed to meet for lunch. She brought two of her current teammates with her.

There was no pitch deck. No presentation. Just iced water sweating onto the wooden table, the sound of silverware shifting in the background, my belief that local mattered, and a straightforward talk about how the work actually gets done — who keeps what, what support really looks like, and how to build a business that serves your life instead of consuming it.

Becky and her teammates listened — curious but guarded. "I'll think about it," she said.

Not long after, my phone rang again and I saw Becky's name on the screen.

"Josh, it's Becky. Let's do it."

On June 6, 2018, she transferred her license to Raeco.

Her yes wasn't loud or dramatic. It was thoughtful. It was steady. It was hers.

STARTING WHERE SHE WAS

When I first reached out to Becky, she was a year into real estate and already had a reputation for being professional, steady, and client-first. But she was feeling the same pressure many good agents feel and had realized the math of the Big Box model didn't match the effort she put in. High splits, higher team share, and little clarity on what she was getting in return wasn't what she wanted for her career long-term.

After she said yes to Raeco, she chose to join on our safer onramp, Plan B compensation. She was still working a second job as a waitress and knew that leaving what she already knew at the Big Box brokerage was a risk, so easing into Raeco on our Plan B roadmap was the option that fit where she was in life.

Six months later, her volume rose. The numbers tapped her on the shoulder, and she realized the conservative choice was starting to cost her. It was time to make another pivot.

With a yellow legal pad covered in circles, arrows, and numbers only we could interpret between us, Becky said, "Plan A seems obvious, but it's still scary."

On January 1, 2019, she switched to Plan A. It wasn't a grand gesture. It was simply the right next step. That same season, she made another call that looks simple on paper but feels massive in real life: She quit serving after thirteen years in the restaurant industry.

"I had to give real estate full gas," she said.

That line stuck with me because it wasn't a slogan. It was a decision about who she was going to be at 8:00 a.m., 2:00 p.m., and 7:00 p.m. It was commitment disguised as courage.

Momentum followed and did what momentum does.

A friend got licensed and asked about joining her.

Then another person asked about her switch to Raeco.

When reflecting on this period, she laughed and said, "I never wanted a team. But I thought, *What the hell?*"

That's how leadership usually starts. You don't wake up one morning a team leader; you just start answering bigger questions about capacity, standards, and service quality. Caring enough to consistently answer those questions *is* leadership.

By the end of 2020, Becky had hit the ridge line every successful agent eventually reaches. And to put it into her words, she had too many "tables," not enough hands.

"If you have too many tables, you're in the weeds, and you end up giving bad service," she said. "I knew I needed a back server — someone to keep me out of the weeds."

So she hired Adriane as an assistant.

Calls got returned faster.

Files stayed clean.

Clients felt the difference.

Becky's sales nearly doubled.

When leverage is right, it doesn't just give you hours back. It gives you the right hours back — the hours when only *you* can do the work.

THE OPERATING SYSTEM

The business choices Becky made only make sense once you understand the culture underneath them. She's community-minded in a way that isn't performative. She sponsors local nonprofits and youth teams. She hires local vendors even when national ones are cheaper. Those aren't random acts of charity; they're strategy that feels like service.

If you've ever worked a Habitat for Humanity build, you know the feeling. The sun's barely up and already warm on your neck. Sawdust fills the air. You're holding a wall straight while someone else drives nails, and the future homeowner is right there smiling. Becky was there too. Days like that aren't a photo-op; they're a good day's work for someone who deserves a home.

That kind of calendar entry is the kind that changes the person who shows up to work Monday. And **that** is where Raeco's Noble Vision really lives.

When I talk about our "Noble Vision," I'm talking about more than a business plan. It's a picture of success that doesn't force you to trade income for family or production for community. My goal is to build and foster a company where the work you do actually shows up in your paycheck, where decisions are made locally, and where what you're building feels like home.

Real camaraderie isn't a fantasy. I'd seen glimpses of that warmth before in my Big Box days, and I knew if connection could exist inside a franchise, then going all-in on local should make connection the central operating system.

This culture wasn't something we just wrote on a wall and hoped it worked out. It's the culture expressed in the ordinary Tuesday decisions — who we hire, who we help, how we show up. And Becky embodied that long before either of us realized where her path was heading.

YOUR PATH TO REAL SUCCESS

It's tempting to make all this sound inevitable when it's written down. But I assure you, it wasn't. Becky's success was a sequence we mapped and she committed to walking:

- Spring 2018: The first call.
- May 2018: The lunch meeting.
- June 2018: License transfer and Plan B.
- January 2019: Switch to Plan A.
- December 2019: Launch a team.
- November 2020: Hire an assistant.

From there she grew to seven agents, became one of the top 10 in her market, and started taking on flips and rentals. Every step was scary until it wasn't. But the more she aligned her model with the math — and the math with her values — the simpler it all became.

If you're an agent reading this, independence isn't a magic trick. It's simply a clearer path. Keep more of what you earn. Ask for help down the hall and get it the same day. Build your own brand — #BeckySoldIt, in Becky's case — instead of borrowing someone else's. Be local on purpose.

And maybe, in your own way, you're standing where Becky once stood. Maybe you're a year or two into your role, working hard and doing everything right, but feeling like the math isn't matching your effort. Maybe you're on a team that looks successful from the outside, but the split feels heavier every month and you're not sure what you're actually getting in return.

Maybe you're established and you have a solid reputation and steady clients, but you're quietly wondering why your income hasn't grown with your skill. Or maybe you're loyal, committed, and grateful for where you've been, but something in your gut knows you're outgrowing the system you're in.

Wherever you are, just know this: **Becky didn't make one enormous leap. She made a series of honest, responsible decisions that aligned her model with her values. You can do the same.**

Familiarity feels safe when your calendar's full and the logo on your card feels like armor. But independence isn't exposure; it's ownership. Gross numbers look impressive on a flyer, but the net income pays for dinner with your kids.

And if Becky's story stirred something in you — even a small curiosity — pay attention to that. It's often the first sign that something better is possible.

WHAT WE'RE REALLY BUILDING

Connection isn't an accident. You can build it on purpose. Our job at Raeco is to make it the default — and then go further. We throw our weight into local, make decisions here, and know each other well enough to do better work together than we could alone.

That's the Noble Vision: a company where agents keep more of what they earn, where help is close, where your brand looks like you, and where your calendar includes ribbon cuttings and volunteer days.

When I first left Becky that voicemail, I didn't know it, but she would become one of the clearest pictures of what real success looks like when you're business-aligned, autonomous, and deeply connected to your community. And the reason her story matters is because real success can look the same for you.

If you remember one line from this chapter, let it be Becky's declaration: "I had to give real estate full gas."

That's what real success looks like. It's steady hands on the wheel, courage in motion, and a company built to keep you connected to the place you call home.

And whether your path leads you to start something of your own or to simply find a local brokerage aligned with your values, my hope is that this book gives you the clarity, tools, and confidence to take your next step.

CHAPTER 3

THE ST. ELMO DIFFERENCE

"Independent companies like ours play a different game. We're not beholden to shareholders or quarterly earnings calls — we're accountable to our agents, clients, and communities. That freedom allows us to stay true to our values and put people before profits."

— **OB Jacobi, President, Windermere Real Estate**

It wasn't real estate that first taught me what great standards feel like. It was a restaurant. And a shrimp cocktail.

Before Raeco Realty ever existed, my life ran on ticket times and table turns. I was the general manager at Walt's Other Pub, a well-loved local spot that felt like the Cheers of our town, where the owner knew your name, your favorite drink, and probably your kid's batting average or how many yards they ran that touchdown for last Friday night. The days were long, I wore the same black shoes every day, and a server pad lived in my back pocket.

Walt's taught me that "being local" really means belonging, being known, and showing up. Interestingly, it was a legendary restaurant in downtown Indianapolis that taught me what *standards* meant. It was a lesson burned so deep that I can still feel the sting today.

THE ST. ELMO EXPERIENCE

As the general manager of Walt's, I worked closely with vendors and distributors all the time, so a dinner invitation wasn't unusual. But an invite from a vendor rep to St. Elmo Steak House? That was unique. This wasn't just any restaurant — it was an Indianapolis landmark every Hoosier knows by name. This woman was one of those seasoned reps who seemed to know every restaurateur within a hundred miles, and she knew I'd appreciate this place.

I'd heard the stories about the shrimp cocktail that makes your eyes water; the wood-paneled walls that have seen every deal, every anniversary, every handshake; and the famous guests from all around the world, but this was my first visit to St. Elmo.

If you're not from Indiana or have never heard of St. Elmo Steak House, think of the kind of century-old restaurant people will literally book flights for. The kind of place where the reservation is part of the celebration and just being there makes you sit up a little straighter.

The moment we stepped inside, the atmosphere wrapped around us — warm, steady, and confident. Not loud, just a low thrum like a well-tuned engine. The wood seemed to remember every story shared by every table of patrons it had ever hosted. The air carried the smell of steak, cherry and vanilla from the bar, and that razor-sharp edge of fresh horseradish that warned you: **Standards are about to be enforced.**

"Shrimp cocktail," my rep said, grinning. "Trust me."

I didn't even like shrimp. But this was *the* thing. You can't walk into a room that proud of its signature dish and skip it. The server placed it in front of me with the famous warning. I nodded, took a big bite, and then it hit.

Fire through the eyes and over the bridge of my nose. No thoughts, just heat. Then clarity.

It wasn't pain; it was cleansing. Like someone opened a window in the back of my head and let the fresh air rush in.

TWO KINDS OF BUSINESSES

As the burn faded, I started to *see* differently. The details stood out — the choreography of it all. Plates landing at once. A water glass topped up without a word. A regular sitting down, and their drink just appearing. A manager in a dark suit scanning the room — not hovering, just keeping tempo.

Everything ran with purpose.

You can walk outside of St. Elmo and see the neon glow of chain restaurants down the block. You already know their menus, prices, and same "not bad" food you forget by morning.

But St. Elmo? This place was special. I could feel it.

That's when the picture snapped into focus and I realized there are two kinds of businesses

> There are two kinds of businesses in this world: One optimizes for being the same *everywhere*. The other optimizes for being *unmistakable somewhere.*

in this world: One optimizes for being the same *everywhere*. The other optimizes for being *unmistakable somewhere*.

Back then, I didn't realize how much that thought would shape the rest of my career. I just knew I wanted to run a business that felt like *that room*.

WHEN THE METAPHOR BECOMES THE MODEL

Years later, after Raeco Realty was born, I'd sit through pitches from national platforms promising reach, efficiency, and automation. I'd nod politely and feel that St. Elmo's door handle in my palm again.

They'd talk about standardization, and I'd remember the shrimp cocktail that refused to please everyone.

They'd promise scalability, and I'd think about that manager who knew every name in the room.

They'd show me charts about leads and platforms, and I'd picture the glow of the chain restaurants visible from the awning-covered front door of St. Elmo and how easily forgettable they felt.

On paper, the old corporate model in real estate made perfect sense. It solved problems that used to be expensive, like software, training, and compliance. Big brands were once the only way to get those tools.

But then, quietly — and then all at once — the ground shifted.

Technology leveled the field. Design went from someone else's print shop to templates you could personalize on your laptop at home. Training moved from ballrooms to bite-sized workshops you could apply next week. Consumers stopped asking, "Which brand?" and started asking, "Which *person*?" They began watching response times, checking online reviews, and trusting recommendations from their local networks. The advantage slid from the logo to the local.

That's when I realized that tools are table stakes and standards are what set you apart. St. Elmo stopped being a metaphor for exceptional service and became a blueprint. I didn't want to build a kitchen designed for a billion identical burgers. I wanted a dining room where people are known by name, the sauce makes your eyes water, and the service is unforgettable.

In real estate terms, that meant building a brokerage that's *famous somewhere* — and maybe, eventually, known everywhere. In that order.

That decision shows up in my work every day. And the difference isn't theoretical; it impacts our clients, team members, and the company. Here's how:

- **For buyers:** The "same everywhere" model can feel like working with call centers, drip campaigns, scripts, and whoever's next in the rotation. The "unmistakable somewhere" model feels like a neighbor picking you up at the airport because you're flying into a new city you're hoping to call home, showing up to meet you with your favorite coffee, or just telling you the truth *before* you even ask. One is a process. The other is a relationship.
- **For agents:** In the old model, you're often a line item in someone else's growth chart. The requirements to be there are generally a heartbeat and a license. Your production matters; *you* don't always. In the new model, you're known by name and story. And even more importantly, the owner knows the same details about your spouse and

kids. Your standards actually shape the company. You're not just using the tools; you help decide which tools exist.
- **For the business itself:** A "same everywhere" brokerage can scale fast, but it can also vanish fast. If the sign changes, the heartbeat barely skips a beat. A business built on standards creates gravity. People feel it when they walk in and they talk about it when they leave. That doesn't just survive; it compounds.

One approach sells reach. The other builds trust.

CULTURE IS A STANDARD

Another way that the *unmistakable somewhere* approach impacts the real estate industry is in recruiting. A big head count looks good on a presentation slide, but it doesn't build a standard.

I've said no to agents who would've made our month because I've seen what happens when you seat the wrong table. One loud, wrong-fit person can ruin the tone of the room. Culture isn't a slogan. It's a standard you protect.

Community spending is another area impacted by the choice between *unmistakable somewhere* and *same everywhere*. A national model often ships its marketing dollars out of town. We try to write checks to our local Little League teams, booster clubs, bakeries, builder dinners, and nonprofits. Folks in your community see you living out the promise to support local and they feel it in their day-to-day interactions. That's how you build a business that people are proud to belong to.

People often tell me, "Big is safe." And I get it. There's comfort in the laminated playbook. You can predict, you can hide. But you don't build a St. Elmo by hiding.

That restaurant isn't famous because it tried to be everywhere. It's famous because it refused to stop being itself right where it was.

The shrimp cocktail isn't for everyone — and that's the point. Standards that please everyone stand for nothing.

Real estate began as a community business. The broker wasn't just a business owner — they helped shape the town. They knew the shortcuts around town, the school secretaries, and the inspectors who overwrote every report. Then the industry drifted corporate because technology rewarded the biggest checkbook.

Now, the map's flipped back. The tools are equal, your website and social media are your front door, and what matters most is what mattered a hundred years ago: Are you there for people? Do you tell the truth even when it costs you? Do your decisions make your town better?

We're not perfect. We miss calls. We tweak listings. But when something breaks, we don't need a plane ticket to fix it. At Raeco, we're close to the ground, and that closeness attracts the right people: agents who want a standard and clients who want truth.

If you want to know if you're working close to the ground in your community, ask yourself, "If the money our agents generate left our region tomorrow, who would miss it?"

I want the answer to be *a lot of people.*

That's not branding. That's a gut check. And it's a question worth asking yourself about where you hang your license right now.

STANDARDS OVER SCALE

Over the years, multiple Big Box brokerages have tried to buy Raeco. They preach standardization and being identical in every market.

That chain restaurant's glowing lights a block away from St. Elmo? Nobody flies to Indianapolis for that place. They fly in and book a table where the standards are old and kept. That's the whole ballgame, and I knew I'd choose *unmistakable somewhere* over *same everywhere* every time I had the chance.

If you're an agent wondering whether to make a change, try this quick truth test I run on myself:

1. If your corporate sign came down tomorrow, would your clients still call you?
2. When you need something fixed, do you talk to a person who actually has the authority to fix it? How many layers of leadership does the problem have to climb before it gets fixed?
3. Do your leaders know your true bottlenecks and goals, or just your numbers?
4. When you look at your commission check, do you feel paid for your value? Or do you feel like you're paying for someone else's overhead?
5. Can you build your version of St. Elmo inside the kitchen you're currently in?

If those questions sting a little, good. That's clarity. I'm not telling you to burn the boats, I'm just encouraging you to be intentional about where you choose to hang your sign.

The old way confuses scale with service. It's very good at looking busy. The new way is quieter — and harder. It demands standards you can taste and a willingness to be known right where you live.

It asks you to trade shortcuts for something heavier: truth.

YOUR NEXT STEP

That night at St. Elmo Steak House still lingers with me. I was young, riding along on someone else's tab, and watching a dining room that ran like it had a soul. That first bite was followed by shock, then clarity.

That's what a real standard does. It burns through the noise and shows you the next step. For me, that step was Raeco Realty. For you, it might be something different, but it'll be *yours*.

Build a business that belongs to your place. Answer the phone. Keep your promises when nobody's looking. Set a few simple, stubborn standards and defend them.

Do that long enough, and your reputation will travel.

Famous everywhere is a mirage if you're not unmistakable somewhere.

CHAPTER 4

THE COST OF COMFORT

"Why am I still here?"

Grant's Coke with grenadine sat between us, the condensation leaving another perfect circle next to the 11 already on the table. The lunch rush had long faded, replaced by the low clatter of dishes from the kitchen and the echoes of a few lingering conversations. Sunlight peeked through the front windows, catching the motion of someone passing by on the sidewalk outside, a delivery truck easing into a spot, and a car door shutting. Inside, the world felt still.

We'd been here for hours. The waitress had stopped asking if we needed anything, just slid by with that look that said she was ready for us to wrap it up. The table was covered in notes, numbers, systems, ideas, and half-formed diagrams scratched down onto paper that started to look more like a football playbook than a business plan.

Grant leaned forward, tracing the edge of one of the water rings with his finger. "I just don't know," he said quietly. "Maybe I'm fine where I'm at."

Every agent says that at least once. Maybe you've said it too. The Big Box office feels familiar. The logo looks safe. The paychecks come steady enough to quiet the questions. But what if staying still is what's actually holding you back?

For a moment, neither of us spoke. The light shifted on the table, and I could see him turning the thought over in his mind — the possibility that *fine* might be the most expensive word in his business.

Grant and I had worked together for years at our old brokerage. We were proud of what we'd built there, but once Sherrie sold the company and the new ownership stepped in, the heart of the business changed and the culture felt hollow. I hadn't yet handed in my resignation, but it was coming. And I was already laying the foundation that would eventually become Raeco. All I needed was someone who believed in the vision for building something local as much as I did.

Grant's hesitation wasn't emotional; it was practical. He wanted to see the data that supported his belief that local could be better. "I'm not afraid of change," he said, "but I'm not going to jump just because it sounds good. Show me the math."

So we ran all the numbers — splits, fees, marketing costs, technology expenses, the works. The table scratch between us told the truth neither of us could ignore. His so-called *comfort* was costing him thousands a year.

That realization didn't make the decision for him, but it cracked the door open. He wasn't just asking, "Can I make this move?" anymore. He was asking, "Why am I still here?"

A few days later, I was in my office at the old brokerage quietly getting things ready for the transition when Grant walked in, shut the door behind him, and said, "I'm in."

There was no second-guessing. I was leaving Big Box to start something local, and he was doing it with me.

BUILDING SOMETHING BETTER

When the doors to Raeco opened, Grant was the first agent to come on board. We didn't call him Agent #1 because that's not how we see people, but he was the first to take the leap with me and transfer his license to our new venture. He was followed shortly thereafter by my old team lead, Christine. Together, we set up systems, vendors, and support tools while still helping clients every day. They asked good questions, offered better ideas, and cared about getting things right. There was no manual, no safety net — just shared belief and hard work.

Even after the paperwork was signed, there were still unknowns. Grant looked at me one afternoon and said, "It's weird — I've always had a company telling me how things are supposed to work. Now I get to help decide how they work."

That shift took a little getting used to, but once it clicked, everything started moving faster. If a system didn't fit, we fixed it. If an agent needed something, we handled it that day. No waiting. No tickets. No layers of approval.

Within months, he realized his business hadn't paused; it had grown. The freedom to move quickly, make decisions locally, and keep more of what he earned created momentum that just wasn't possible before. And his growth wasn't just about money. It was about a renewed sense of belonging to something you help build.

One day, after we'd wrapped up another conversation about recruiting and operations, Grant leaned back in his chair and laughed. "I honestly don't get it," he said. "I don't understand why agents stay where they are. Why don't they do the math?"

That line has stuck with me, and I often still hear Grant repeat it to this day. It's the real question under every hesitation. Why do good agents settle for less — less input, less income, less connection — just because it feels familiar?

Grant had gone from cautious to confident. From calculating risk to championing change. The same man who once said, "Maybe I'm fine where I'm at," was now living proof that *fine* is the real risk.

Since then, Grant's become a cornerstone of Raeco. He helps wherever help is needed — training new agents, supporting community projects, and even stepping into leadership roles in our local association. He's known in town not just as a successful agent, but as someone who makes real estate better for everyone around him. He's proof that switching brokerages doesn't mean starting over; it means starting stronger.

WHY YOU STAY WHERE YOU ARE

If you think you're "fine" where you're at, there's a good chance you're actually stuck. This chapter is about showing you what staying still is really costing you — and how to recognize when it's time to move.

Most agents don't stay put because they're lazy. They stay because of the stories they've been told (and retold) about what's safe, what's risky, and what's "just the way things are." Let's name a few of those myths and then pull them apart.

Myth 1: All Brokerages Are Basically the Same

This might be the costliest belief in the industry. On the surface, sure, every brokerage has listings, signs, a logo, and maybe even a training calendar and a tech stack. But under the hood, there's a dramatic difference between a Big Box enterprise and a local agency.

Here are seven differences Grant and I discovered firsthand:

1. **Decision-making speed and location.** Local means faster. When the owners live nearby, problems get solved in hours, not weeks.
2. **Commission structures and hidden fees.** Transparency matters. The money you keep should reflect the value you create, not what someone else dictates.
3. **Marketing support quality.** Local teams know your market better than any national template ever could.
4. **Community involvement.** Big brands talk about giving back. Local brokerages actually show up with time, money, and a helping hand.

5. **Agent input in direction.** Your voice matters when leadership sits across the same table, not in another state.
6. **Training and mentorship.** Smaller brokerages tailor growth to your goals, not a one-size-fits-all program.
7. **Culture and values alignment.** When the people around you share your values, work feels lighter and wins feel personal.

These aren't small differences. They're the difference between being managed and being mentored.

Myth 2: Switching Brokerages Will Disrupt My Business

Believing this myth sounds like responsible thinking, but it's usually a fear that someone else told you or put into your head. Yes, if you jump without a plan, you can create chaos. But done right, a transition doesn't have to skip a beat.

When Grant moved, his deals never paused. We handled the paperwork, the branding, the signs, and the behind-the-scenes details so his clients barely noticed the change (other than the fact that he seemed more energized and more in control).

The real disruption isn't switching brokerages. It's staying in a model that slowly drains your margin, your energy, and your belief.

Myth 3: Clients Only Trust Big Brands

The reality is that clients follow *people*, not logos.

Think about your own referrals. When someone says, "You have to call my agent," they rarely mention your brokerage first. They talk about how you answered your phone, negotiated like crazy, or sat with them in a cold kitchen at 9:00 p.m. to talk through an inspection report.

Local trust runs deeper than any national slogan. A big brand might get you a glance, but your reputation closes the gap.

Myth 4: Independence Is Lonely

This one keeps a lot of good agents from making moves they've already decided they want to make. Independence doesn't mean isolation. The right local brokerage gives you more ownership and more belonging. You're surrounded by people who chose that environment for the same reason you're considering it now.

With a local brokerage, it's not, "Good luck, you're on your own." It's, "You're the driver of your business and we're here to help in any way we can."

THE "I'M FINE" TRAP

Comfort whispers in your ear and tells you that you're doing fine. It's quiet. It's convincing. But it's expensive.

Grant thought he was fine too — until he saw what "fine" was costing him in income, influence, and impact. Staying put trades growth for predictability and passion for routine. So, ask yourself:

- Am I actually fine, or just familiar?
- Does my company invest in my community, or just cash my checks?
- If leadership changed tomorrow, would my business feel it, or would nothing change at all?

Once you've answered these questions honestly, test the data just like Grant did.

- **Run the numbers.** Pull the financials from your last 12 months. What did you gross? What did you net after splits, fees, and extras? Then ask yourself, "If my structure were different, how much of that could I have kept?"
- **Check your influence.** When you have an idea, does anyone listen? Do you have a say in how your brokerage grows and serves clients, or are you just expected to plug into someone else's vision?
- **Look at your community footprint.** Where does your company actually show up? Sponsorships, events, volunteer days — does your logo stand next to things you're proud of, or does it mostly live on yard signs and flyers?

If that little self-audit makes you pause, it might be time to take a harder look at what "fine" is costing you.

WHY YOUR CHOICE MATTERS

Grant's story isn't about luck. It's about clarity. He didn't leave the Big Box model because he was miserable; he left because he finally saw what was possible — and what staying put was really costing him.

The truth is, you're not broken. You're just operating inside a system that quietly rewards you for staying small and quiet. Comfort feels safe until you realize the bill it's been racking up behind the scenes. Once you see that, change doesn't feel reckless anymore. It feels overdue.

My hope is that this chapter gives you language for the restlessness you've been feeling and a few simple self-assessments you can use to measure your own career. You don't have to blow anything up tomorrow. But you *do* owe it to yourself, your family, and your community to at least do the math, ask better questions, and be honest about whether "fine" is still good enough.

Because on the other side of "I'm fine where I'm at" is where your real career begins.

CHAPTER 5

THE FIVE PILLARS THAT CHANGE EVERYTHING

The room felt more like a classroom than a mastermind, and in a lot of ways, it was exactly that for me. I'd just started Raeco Realty and was the new guy in the broker-owner meeting at our local Association of REALTORS® office. I knew a couple of the other leaders well, like Cheryl, my former managing broker, but most of the others I only knew by name. There was a quiet buzz of conversation as people took their seats, and though I wasn't exactly nervous, there was a sense of being the newcomer stepping into a long-established circle.

I found an open seat near the middle of the room and was getting settled when Charlie Shook walked in. He looked around, smiled, and made his way directly toward me. Without hesitation, he sat down next to the new guy.

He introduced himself like we hadn't met before, handed me his card, and said, "If you ever need anything while you're getting up and running, call me."

That single gesture hit harder than any lecture or leadership seminar ever could. Here was a respected industry leader showing generosity to someone who was technically the competition. Charlie's words from his keynote delivered in the Purdue ballroom echoed again: "In this business, your competition becomes your coworker as you work side by side to get the transaction closed — and by the end of it, that coworker often becomes your friend."

Right there, it clicked. Leadership wasn't about territory or titles; it was about values in action. I felt an energized clarity wash over me. This was the kind of leader I wanted to be. The kind of company I wanted to build. A place where people came before profit and where generosity wasn't a strategy but a standard.

Clear values create confident decisions. When you intentionally define and live by your values, every choice in your business becomes easier, faster, and more aligned. In this chapter, I'm going to walk you through the five pillars that guide Raeco and show you how to use them as a filter for your own career, no matter where you're working today.

Our values didn't come out of a corporate handbook. They were forged through late-night talks, tough decisions, and conversations that mattered — with Cassie at our kitchen counter, with Christine over coffee, and with Grant in the middle of one of those 11:00 p.m. text threads that start with, "What if we tried…"

As Raeco grew, more and more agents began to help align my values into five clear principles that became our DNA. They guide every check we write, every person we hire, every decision we make.

Around here, we call them **the five pillars.**

PILLAR 1: PEOPLE OVER PROFIT

When we brought on Nelson Pelton — our in-house marketing guru — it was one of the biggest leaps of faith we've taken as a company. Nelson owned his own business, Octothorpe Media, which he had built from the ground up. His company produced some of the best real estate marketing in town. I'd been using him since his early days as a company, when Raeco was hardly even recognized as a brand.

By the time we had the conversation about what it would look like for Nelson to join the Raeco team, Nelson had hit a wall. He was burned out, shooting for 56 agents across multiple companies who were all expecting next-day turnarounds on photos and videos. After a few honest conversations over coffee, I knew what needed to happen. I made him an offer to come join the Raeco family. Having Nelson on board would give our agents exclusive access to his services and give him the balance and partnership he needed to keep doing what he loved.

There was only one problem: His salary was higher than what the brokerage was making at the time. The math said no, but my gut said yes. I knew my personal commissions could cover the difference, so I took the gamble and offered him the job.

As I believed, it was the right move for our agents, for the company, and for the brand. Nelson became a huge asset. Bringing him in reminded me that leadership really means giving our agents what they need to succeed.

Key Principle

Agents are the clients of the local brokerage. With that in mind, I believe that to do it right, every decision should start with the question, "What can we do to help you?" If the answer costs us more today but makes our agents stronger tomorrow, we do it.

How to Apply This Pillar

You don't have to own a brokerage to live the people-over-profit mindset. Here are some ways you can apply this approach, no matter who you are:

- **If you're an agent on a team or at a Big Box:** Start by treating *your clients* with the people-over-profit mindset. Look at your next three decisions — about pricing, marketing, or time — and ask, "What would I do if I put their best interest first, not my convenience?" Then actually do it and watch what it does to your referrals and repeat business.
- **If you're a team lead or an aspiring broker-owner:** Treat your agents the way you traditionally treat your buyers and sellers. Where are they jammed up? What problems are costing them time, energy, or money that you could solve — even if it hits your short-term margin? Your people will remember who paid the bill when it mattered.

When you're thinking about how to adopt this people-over-profit mindset, start by auditing who you're really serving. Grab a sheet of paper and make two columns. In

Column A, list the things you do because "that's the way we do it here." In Column B, list the things you do because it's genuinely best for your client. Anything in Column A that contradicts Column B is a place to lead, even if your company doesn't. Over time, people over profit becomes your reputation and your competitive advantage.

PILLAR 2: ROOTED IN LOCAL, DRIVEN BY COMMUNITY

Shortly after Raeco opened our second office in Delphi, Indiana, I handed a set of keys to the local Chamber of Commerce and the local Economic Development Corporation. Both groups occasionally needed a larger meeting space, and our conference room was perfect for it. It was a simple move that turned into a win-win. They got a space that fit their needs, and we got the right people walking through our doors and in front of our logo.

That's the heart of what we do: filling community gaps whenever we can. Another way we do this is by trading Nelson's media services — photography, videography, drone work, and graphic design — in exchange for sponsorships. Many nonprofits and community fundraisers can't afford those services, and we have them. Like sharing our space with local organizations, it's a win-win every time.

Key Principle

Live where you work and give where you live.

How to Apply This Pillar

You don't need your name on a building to be rooted locally. When your community sees you as a contributor, not just a salesperson, your career stops being just a job and starts becoming part of the fabric of where you live. Here are four strategies you can use to make an impact in your community by sharing what you have:

1. **Map your community footprint.** List the events, nonprofits, schools, and small businesses that genuinely matter to you. Circle one or two you'd like to build a deeper relationship with, not just slap your logo on their banner.
2. **Trade what you're good at.** Maybe you don't have a big sponsorship budget yet. That's fine. You have time, relationships, and skills. Offer to help a local nonprofit with open houses, event check-in, or promotions. Show up consistently and you will be remembered.
3. **Align your marketing with your zip code.** Before you sign the next marketing contract, ask, "How much of this money stays in my community?" When possible, hire local photographers, printers, sign companies, and caterers. Your dollars build your own farm.
4. **Use real estate as a bridge, not just a business.** Invite clients to local events, promote neighborhood fundraisers in your newsletter, and become the person people text when they're trying to figure out who to call for anything local.

PILLAR 3: BUILT TOGETHER

One of my favorite parts of leading Raeco is watching how ideas grow when they come from the group. One year, we made the decision to change our transaction management software to something that integrated with our commission platform. On paper, it sounded perfect. In practice, it was a nightmare. The new software caused endless issues, frustrated our agents, and created more problems than it solved.

Adoption tanked, and Cassie, who handles most of our systems, was beside herself when I told her we'd spent $6,000 on a product we weren't even going to use two weeks after we'd bought it. But she knew that the right tools help agents succeed, and we both agreed that we had to make the switch back.

That decision cost us money, but we gained something far more valuable: trust. It showed our team that we listen and that their experience matters. That moment became a blueprint for how we operate.

Key Principle

Make decisions with key stakeholders instead of outsourcing problems to a distant executive team who might not have ever met your agents.

How to Apply This Pillar

Even if you're in a huge corporate system, you can build your *own* "built together" culture. Here's how:

- **Create your own feedback loop.** If you're a solo agent, your team might be your lender, title rep, and favorite inspector. Once a quarter, ask them, "What's one thing we could do differently to make deals smoother?" Then implement one of their suggestions.
- **Hold a simple, monthly check-in with your team or peers.** If you lead others (officially or unofficially), ask about what's working, what's

frustrating, and what everyone needs from leadership that they're not getting. Then, send a summarized version of that feedback up the chain. You might not win every battle, but you'll become the person who advocates thoughtfully, and people remember that.
- **Test and adjust.** When you try a new product, system, or marketing piece, tell your people, "This is a trial. If it doesn't help, we'll pivot." When you *do* pivot, say, "We switched because you spoke up." That sentence alone builds trust.

"Built together" doesn't require a certain logo. It requires the humility to admit when something isn't working and the courage to change it with your people, not for them.

PILLAR 4: EXCELLENCE IN ALL WE DO

There was a time when our marketing budget conversation hit a wall. Someone — usually Cassie, the planner in our duo — asked, "Where's the money going to come from?"

I said, "I don't care where it comes from, we're not cutting corners."

I believe agents deserve the best tools and presentation because their clients deserve the best representation. Because of that, we made the call to double down on excellence by upgrading our branding, photography, and training resources. It meant tighter margins in the short term, but the long-term results spoke for themselves. Listings started standing out more. Our agents gained confidence. The community noticed.

Excellence isn't about being flashy; it's about being intentional. It's the way we answer the phone, the accuracy in our contracts, the quality of our marketing materials, and the respect we show to every client. It's how we show up when no one's watching.

Key Principle

Agents deserve the best opportunities, resources, and tools to represent their clients with pride.

How to Apply This Pillar

You can start living excellence tomorrow with what you already have. Here's how:

- **Run the "Would I send this to my mom?" test.** Look at your last listing photos, your last email to a client, and your voicemail greeting. Would you be proud to send that to your parents? If not, that's where to upgrade first.
- **Pick one upgrade per quarter.** Don't try to overhaul everything at once. Excellence is built by stacking small upgrades consistently, so choose one thing to focus on at a time. For example:
  - Q1: Professional headshots or branding.
  - Q2: Standardize your listing prep checklist.
  - Q3: Upgrade your buyer or seller guide.
  - Q4: Dial in your contract and communication systems.
- **Practice promoting excellence in the invisible.** Double-check your contracts. Show up five minutes early. Send recaps after key conversations. These acts aren't glamorous, but they separate you from 90 percent of the market.
- **Choose not to cut corners, even if your current brokerage does.** You can choose to be the agent

whose listings *always* look good, whose files are *always* clean, and whose communication is *always* clear. That brand will follow you, no matter where you're licensed.

Excellence costs more in the moment, but mediocrity costs your reputation, and that's the most expensive bill there is.

PILLAR 5: HUMBLE, HUNGRY, AND ALWAYS LEARNING

Having trusted mentors in your corner is one of the most important parts of growth. These are the people you can be open and honest with — the ones who tell you the truth even when it stings a little. They're sounding boards, truth-tellers, and friends who help you see what you might be missing.

I've been blessed with incredible mentors throughout my journey — Andy Beery, John Hatter, John Thompson, Scott "Roadie" Ahlersmeyer, and Walt Foster. Each of them opened my eyes to different lessons about leadership, business, and life. Andy continues to challenge how I think about growth and leadership; John Hatter gives me unfiltered truth, business wisdom, and life advice; John Thompson taught me faith, generosity, and what it means to give back quietly; Roadie showed me how to lead by example and that no matter what goes wrong, the show goes on; and Walt showed me what it looks like to truly know your people and be a community business.

This pillar is essential because I think it's probably one of the most important things you can do in business, and it's the foundation of adopting an always-learning mindset. Surround yourself with the right people and you'll be amazed at what can happen.

If you take nothing else from this whole book, find yourself a good mentor. Someone you can trust who will challenge you, support you, and help you grow into the leader you're meant to be.

Early on, I thought I knew it all. I'd run teams, managed people, and launched a company. But my mentors reminded me that growth only happens when you stay teachable. Because of that, I've made it a habit to invest in myself — to hire coaches, attend workshops, and constantly pursue new perspectives that make me a better leader for my team.

Breakfasts with my friend Hatter at the Tick Tock Tavern have become a tradition. For me, it's half conversation, half getting an MBA in life. We tuck into a corner booth, order coffee, and talk about everything from current deals to decisions made to life lessons. Cassie loves when those breakfasts happen because she knows I'll come back with clarity — and a few things I needed to hear, even though I probably didn't want to.

Key Principle

There's always something to learn from every industry, every leader, and every experience.

How to Apply This Pillar

This is the pillar that guarantees you'll keep growing, no matter what market you're in. Here are four things you need to do to stay humble, hungry, and always learning:

1. **Find your Hatter.** Make a short list of three people in your circle who are ahead of you in some way, be it in production, leadership, or character. Ask one of them to coffee by saying, "I respect how you do X. Could I buy you breakfast and ask a few questions?" You'd be surprised how many say yes.
2. **Block time for learning on your calendar.** If it's not scheduled, it's optional. Make learning non-negotiable by putting a one-hour meeting with yourself on your calendar each week labeled "Career Practice." Use it for:
   - Watching a training.
   - Reviewing what people you look up to are doing.
   - Reading a business or leadership book.
   - Studying your last three wins and losses and asking, "What did I miss?"
3. **Steal ideas from other industries.** Pay attention to how your favorite restaurant, barber, or coffee shop treats people. How do they greet patrons? How do they handle mistakes? How do they follow up? Then ask yourself, "What's the real estate version of that?"
4. **Stay coachable, especially when you're successful.** The most dangerous sentence in your career is "I already know this." When you catch that thought, replace it with, "What could I see here that I've missed before?"

Staying humble keeps you open. Staying hungry keeps you moving forward. If you're both, it's almost impossible *not* to grow.

NOT JUST WORDS ON A WALL

These five pillars aren't slogans. They're the filters through which every decision runs — how we hire, spend, plan, and serve. They show up in check registers and community calendars, in conversations and commitments. If you embrace your own local and client-focused core pillars, your values will show through your people. They'll guide the small, daily choices that define who you are when no one's watching.

You don't have to adopt *our* five pillars word for word. But you do need your own. Because when your values are clear, your decisions get simpler:

- Do I stay or go?
- Do I join this team or that one?
- Do I cut this corner or raise the standard?

The right answer usually lines up with what you already say you believe.

If you're wondering whether your current brokerage truly lives by its values, start by assessing it using these five filters. Where does it shine? Where does it fall short? And just as importantly, where do *you* shine, and where do you want to grow?

CHAPTER 6

THE REAL ESTATE REALITY CHECK

"Help me become the agent I know I can be."

Brooke had been licensed for about a year when she asked if we could meet. She was already showing promise and was sharp, personable, and quick to learn, but she was frustrated. Her brokerage was supposed to be helping her with lead generation and marketing support. Instead, she was getting silence and busywork. Every week felt like she was running errands for other agents instead of building her own business.

At the same time, something new was happening around her. Raeco had just opened an office in Delphi, Indiana, and the town was starting to see the Raeco name everywhere — a new sign downtown on Main Street, banners at community events, and small-town sponsorships that meant something. She told me later that she'd kept noticing our sign on her drive through town. It wasn't flashy; it just looked like something solid was happening there — a company that showed up, invested, and believed local still mattered.

By the time she sat across from me during our first meeting, she was ready. "I just need a place that's going to lift me up," she said, "I need someone who is going to help me become the agent I know I can be."

I've had this same conversation with dozens of agents. Trust me when I tell you that you're not broken, you're just working in systems that don't lift you up. You're paying heavy splits and still building everything alone.

Brooke's story isn't about a dramatic failure that led her to look for a change. It's about a quiet realization that sneaks up on you when you start comparing what you're getting with what you're giving. She wanted support, marketing, and leadership that met her halfway. When she found it with Raeco, her entire career trajectory changed.

And that's what this chapter is about: creating a moment of clarity that allows you to clearly see the gaps in your brokerage's support system so you can find a better way to work.

THE CLARITY CHALLENGE

Give yourself 20 minutes. That's it. Just 20 minutes to take a hard, honest look at where you are right now. This isn't a sales pitch or a pep talk. It's a mirror.

Grab a notebook or open the notes app on your phone and work through these four quick exercises. They're simple, but don't underestimate them. If you do them honestly, they'll give you the same thing they gave

Brooke and so many others: a clear picture of what's actually working, what isn't, and what your current brokerage is really doing for you.

You're about to see your business — and your brokerage — very differently.

Part 1: The Decision Speed Test (≈ 5 Minutes)

Think back to the last time you needed an answer from your brokerage. Maybe you had a contract question, a policy clarification, or a client in the middle of a tense deal who needed an answer *now* — not tomorrow, not Monday.

Now, time the request in your mind. How long did it actually take to get a response? Who did you have to contact? How many emails or calls did it take to get the help you needed?

Most agents discover they wait far more than they realize — sometimes hours, sometimes days. And in real estate, hours matter. A delayed answer can mean a delayed offer, a lost client, or a weekend of second-guessing.

Ask yourself:

- How often do I find myself waiting for answers?
- What decisions could I have made in that waiting time?
- How many deals have been slowed down by bureaucratic delays?

When I built Raeco, I wanted that waiting game gone. Our agents can reach leadership directly, and most of the time, they get an answer the same day — often within the hour. I'm not saying this to brag; I'm telling you because *speed is culture*. It reveals how much a company truly values its agents' time.

So as you write down your numbers, look for patterns. If your business runs on someone else's schedule, what is that costing you?

Part 2: The Marketing Reality Check (≈ 8 Minutes)

Now, open the apps where real estate actually lives today, like Instagram, Facebook, or maybe even TikTok. Search your area and look for five to seven agents who are active and visible. Scroll through their feeds, watch their reels, and read their captions.

Take note of what you see. Are they showing up consistently? Are they featuring community events, local businesses, or their own listings? Do their posts make you stop scrolling to engage, or do they all blur together?

Then look at your own social media presence. How often are you posting? What kind of content are you sharing? Would you follow you?

Ask yourself:

- Which agents in my market are clearly standing out, and why?
- What percentage of agents are actually telling a story through their marketing?
- How does my brokerage help (or not help) me show up in the same way?

Most agents find that this quick scroll turns into a reality check. They realize 80 percent of local real estate content looks exactly the same. It's listing photos, "just sold" graphics, and captions with calls to action that say, "Call me for all your real estate needs!"

That sameness isn't lack of effort; it's lack of support. When every post has to fit a corporate brand guide or use preapproved templates, your creativity gets boxed in instead of being leveraged in a way that allows you to stand out.

Brooke saw that difference right away when she came to Raeco. On her old team, she was told what *not* to post. Here, she was encouraged to experiment. She joined a team leader who loved marketing with video tours, short-form reels, and behind-the-scenes stories, and gave her the tools to make it happen. Within weeks, Brooke was posting videos, collaborating on community posts, and seeing her engagement spike. She didn't just "do more marketing," she finally had the space and support to be seen.

You don't have to copy Brooke's strategy, but take an honest look at what's working on social media. In your market, who's actually connecting and who's just checking the box? And where do you fall on that spectrum?

Part 3: The Community Impact Audit (≈ 5 Minutes)

Keep that social media tab open. Now, instead of searching for agents, search for *brokerages* in your area. Scroll through their feeds and look at the company pages, the recruiting accounts, and the corporate profiles. Look at the photos, the videos, and the clips.

In the past year, how many *real* community things have they done? Not just open houses or production awards, but fundraisers, local partnerships, sponsorships, charity drives, chamber events, holiday parades, or school programs. Are they showing up? Are their agents showing up under that same brand banner? Are they sponsoring, attending, or helping in ways that matter to the towns they claim to serve?

Now compare what you find to your own brokerage. Not just what *you* personally do, but your brokerage as an organization (because there's a difference between

having community-minded agents and having a community-minded company).
Ask yourself:

- When my brokerage posts, does it reflect the place I actually live and work?
- Does my company put its name and resources behind local causes with dollars and time, or not at all?
- Does the only community investment happen when individual agents do it on their own?

If your brokerage's social media is mostly national campaigns, awards graphics, or cookie-cutter content from headquarters, that's not connection, that's camouflage.

When Raeco opened in Delphi, one of our first moves wasn't a billboard or a recruiting ad. It was hanging a sign on Main Street downtown and then showing up everywhere that sign could be recognized, like the Chamber of Commerce, Little League events, fundraisers, and local festivals. We weren't hiding because we knew you can't build real trust from a distance.

So take another scroll through your feed. Who's really investing in your community and who's just advertising to it?

Part 4: The True Support Analysis (≈ 2 Minutes)

Create two columns on a piece of paper. Label the first column *What my brokerage does for me*. Then label the second column *What I do myself (that I thought they helped with)*. In each column, jot down items like:

- Marketing creation
- Contract support
- Technology tools
- Training programs

- Administrative tasks
- Problem solving
- Business systems and growth strategies

Now step back. Which column is longer?

For most agents, the second column wins by a landslide. They realize they're the ones designing postcards in Canva at midnight, figuring out client issues that leadership should have helped with, and juggling most of the daily responsibilities that keep their business moving. They're doing 80–90 percent of the work while paying corporate overhead for the illusion of help.

That realization stings, but it's also freeing. Because once you name the gap, you can finally fix it.

When Brooke made her move, she immediately noticed how different *real* support felt. She had direct access to leadership, a marketing team that produced on schedule, and peers who shared ideas instead of guarding them. She went from feeling like a gofer to feeling like a professional.

Ask yourself:

- What am I actually paying for?
- How much of my success is really my own effort?
- What would change if I had genuine support?

Processing the Results

Take a look at everything you just wrote down. You may see patterns like:

- Delays that drain momentum.
- Marketing that blends in instead of stands out.
- A brokerage that's invisible in its own community.
- Support systems that depend on you more than they help you.

Maybe your buyer lost out on a home because you were still waiting on a manager's reply. Maybe your last listing looked just like the one across town because the same stock system produced both. Maybe your company name hasn't appeared at a local fundraiser in years.

If any of that sounds familiar, you're not imagining it. The traditional brokerage model was designed for scale, not agility. It's great at adding offices but not necessarily at adding value.

Brooke discovered that firsthand. She didn't suddenly become a better agent overnight; she simply moved to an environment that amplified her effort instead of absorbing it.

The same is true for most high-performing agents. They're already doing the work — they just need a platform that multiplies it instead of muffling it.

Now that you see the gaps, ask yourself what it would look like:

- If answers came faster so I could run my business the way I wanted?
- If my marketing actually reflected my creativity?
- If my brokerage showed up in my neighborhood?
- If my support team worked as hard for me as I do for my clients?

This version of work isn't a fantasy; it's alignment. When your brokerage's priorities match your own, progress feels lighter. You stop fighting for momentum and start building with it. Clarity doesn't demand that you change tomorrow, it

> When your brokerage's priorities match your own, progress feels lighter.

just makes it impossible to stay comfortable in a situation that's just "fine."

Still, even after seeing these gaps clearly, doubt creeps in. What if change doesn't work out? What if it's just as hard somewhere else? That hesitation is normal — every strong agent I've met has felt it — but doubt isn't danger. Instead, it's a signal that you're standing on the edge of growth.

Before you make any moves, let's talk about those doubts and questions that keep you up at night after reading chapters like this one.

CHAPTER 7

WHEN DOUBT GETS LOUD

"Will this really work For me?"

The glow from the Edison bulbs above the bar cast a soft amber light across the worn brick walls of the Brick & Mortar Pub in Delphi, Indiana. I'd been here plenty of times before, but tonight, the booth across from me carried more weight than usual.

Jess and her husband, Nate, slid into the booth, both still in work mode. Cassie sat beside me, flipping through the drink menu, and we all landed on the same choice: Brick & Mortar's sangria. It's the kind of drink that's made for long conversations and slow decisions.

Jess had just come from a showing and was wearing a blazer over denim with her hair pulled back — that mix of business and exhaustion every agent knows. I'd known her long before either of us carried business cards. Back when Cassie and I lived in our first house in Fiddlesticks, a Lafayette neighborhood, Jess and Nate were our neighbors. Nate ran the HOA there, and Jess was the one waving to us from her driveway while walking her dogs. This wasn't a recruiting dinner. This was a conversation between friends who already trusted each other.

"I know I need to do it," Jess said, swirling the ice cubes in her glass. "It just feels like starting over."

"You're not starting over," I said. "You're starting fresh. There's a difference."

Nate leaned back. "She's doing fine where she is. Clients know her. She's got a rhythm."

"Of course," I said. "The national brands are great at systems. But systems can't see potential. You've been running someone else's playbook for years. Maybe it's time to write your own."

Jess smiled, half tired, half curious. She'd been in real estate since 2017 — around the same time we opened Raeco. She started at a Big Box brokerage, learned under a mentor, joined a team, worked her way up, and was doing well enough to feel safe. But, as you know, that's the most dangerous place in this business: comfortable, competent, and quietly restless.

"What if I make the move and it doesn't work?" she asked. "What if I mess up everything I've built?"

"That's the voice of doubt everyone hears right before they level up," I said. "You get to decide whether you listen to it or not."

The waitress stopped by to clear our plates, but none of us were in a hurry to leave. Outside the window, the dim downtown glow of Delphi's Main Street pressed through the glass, revealing that small-town quiet that settles after the dinner rush.

"I keep thinking about what I could do if I had more creative control," Jess said. "Videos. Local spotlights. Real stuff that connects."

"There it is," I said. "That's you talking, not fear."

She laughed. "Yeah, and then five minutes later I talk myself out of it."

"That's what happens when you're used to someone else calling the shots," I said.

Nate grinned. "He's not wrong."

Jess sighed, but the corners of her mouth softened. "I just need to do it," she said.

I smiled. "You've been saying that for a year. One of these days, *Not yet* is going to turn into *Why didn't I do this sooner?*"

When we finally stood to leave, Jess hugged Cassie and me. "Soon," she said.

I believed her. That night, something had shifted, and I could tell that voice of doubt in Jess's mind just got quieter.

THE DOUBTS EVERY AGENT FACES

If you've ever wondered whether switching brokerages will really work for you, this chapter will help you see the truth behind your doubts. You'll learn why these fears show up, how to move through them, and how agents just like you have made the leap from Big Box brokerages to local brokerages without losing momentum. By the end, you'll understand that doubt isn't a stop sign; it's a signal you're on the edge of growth.

In the months that followed our dinner at Brick & Mortar, Jess and I kept meeting for coffee, exchanging late-night texts, and checking in after closings. Every conversation circled back to the same internal debates I've heard from agents across every Big Box brokerage.

Should I stay?
Should I go?
Am I crazy for even considering this?
If you've been having your own back-and-forth internal battle, you're not alone. These doubts are normal, they're common, and they get a whole lot easier to navigate once someone names them and shows you what's on the other side.

So let's talk about the four big doubts that keep talented and successful agents stuck at Big Box brokerages.

Doubt #1: I Need the National Brand

This one comes up almost every time I speak to an agent about switching to a local operation. Agents feel like the national logo on their business card is what gives them credibility. The truth is that clients don't hire a logo. They hire a person they trust.

One agent told me, "People pick me because I'm with the big company."

"When was the last time a client actually said that?" I asked.

She paused, then laughed and said, "Never."

The comfort of a big name is powerful, but it's also deceptive. That logo can become a security blanket — safe, familiar, and *invisible*. Jess felt the same way. Her clients called her directly; the brand was never part of the conversation. Once she saw that people worked with her because of her reputation, the fear started to fade.

How to Move Past This Doubt

Start with evidence, not assumptions. Think of your last 10 clients. How did they find you? Was it a referral? Social media? An open house? A past relationship?

Now ask yourself honestly: How many of my last 10 clients would have *not* worked with me if my card had a different logo?

If you're like most agents I talk to, the answer is "probably none."

Next, try this simple mental flip: Imagine you left your current brokerage tomorrow but kept your exact same phone number, work ethic, response time, personality, and care for your clients. Would your clients magically stop trusting you? Of course not. They hired *you*.

If you're still nervous, you can take a simple step to test the theory and start subtly building *your* brand alongside your brokerage's. Use consistent colors, fonts, and phrases in your social media. Share your story. Let people connect with your name and face. That way, when you do decide to move, your clients will barely notice the logo change because they were following *you* all along.

Doubt #2: I Don't Deserve Better Support

If you feel this way, you're not alone. This belief sneaks up on experienced agents who've spent years making do. They've been told, "That's just how it is," so many times they start to believe it.

Just before they switched to a local brokerage, one agent told me, "I don't think I've earned help yet."

"If you're closing deals and serving people, you've earned help," I said.

She now has a part-time admin and more time with her family.

Underneath this doubt is a subtle belief: *I'm supposed to struggle.* It's the mindset that if you're tired or overwhelmed, it's just the price of success. Fortunately, that is just a faulty belief that can be overcome.

How to Move Past This Doubt

Start by recognizing the difference between *hard work* and *unnecessary friction*. Ask yourself:

- If my favorite client described me to a friend, what would they say I deserve?
- If my kid or best friend were in my shoes, working as hard as I do, would I tell them, "You haven't earned support yet"?

Then, get specific. Make a quick list of the tasks that drain you most, like:

- Chasing paperwork
- Designing marketing pieces
- Wrestling with tech
- Scheduling and rescheduling

Now, circle the tasks that don't require your license and don't require your unique personality or skill. Those are the areas where you deserve support — today, not someday.

If your current brokerage doesn't offer that kind of help, it doesn't mean you're unworthy of it. It means you're in a system that was never designed to give it. The problem is the structure, not your worth.

You don't have to wait until you're a top producer to ask, "What would it look like to get some help here?" You can start with a shared assistant, a transaction coordinator, or a more supportive environment. You're already carrying more than you think. You're allowed to set some of it down.

Doubt #3: I'm Too Old/New/Different to Succeed Somewhere Else

Real estate loves labels. The veteran thinks they're too old to switch; the rookie thinks they're too green. The introvert worries they're not loud enough; the parent worries they're too busy.

The truth is that adaptability beats age every day.

One of the oldest agents at Raeco came from a corporate office where she felt invisible. She told me, "I figured nobody wants a sixty-year-old learning new tools." Six months later, she was filming walk-through videos — something completely outside her previous comfort zone — and loving it.

How to Move Past This Doubt

Start by naming your "too" belief. For example:

- "I'm too old."
- "I'm too new."
- "I'm too quiet."
- "I'm too different from everyone around me."

Then ask a better question: *For whom?*

Too old for corporate recruiting metrics? Maybe.

Too old to show up as yourself in your own community and build a business on trust and consistency? Absolutely not.

Some of the most successful agents I know started later in life, came from completely different careers, or didn't fit the stereotypical mold of a realtor at all. What they had in common wasn't age or personality type; it was willingness to keep learning and to show up as their real selves.

And actually, if you feel "too new," you have an advantage over people who've been in the industry for years because you have less to unlearn. You don't have 10 years of bad habits to break. In the right environment — with mentorship, systems, and support — you can grow faster than you think.

Try this little exercise:

- Write down three things that make you different from the typical agent in your market.
- For each attribute, write how it could be a *strength* instead of a liability.

Here's what that might look like for you:

- I'm a former teacher. → I'm great at explaining complex things simply.
- I'm not from here originally. → I remember what it's like to be new and can relate to relocation buyers.
- I'm a parent with limited time. → I'm efficient, organized, and deeply respectful of my clients' schedules.

You're not behind. You're just on a path that doesn't match the script you were handed. That's okay. You're allowed to change the script.

Doubt #4: I'm Not Sure I Can Live Up to Higher Standards

This one's tricky because it's actually a compliment in disguise. Agents who struggle with this doubt care deeply about excellence — they just fear exposure. They worry that a smaller, higher-standard brokerage will notice every flaw. The irony is that visibility is what helps them grow.

One agent told me, "At Raeco, I can't hide — but that's what keeps me sharp." A Big Box will make you feel safe because you can hide behind the name, but settling in the shadows will keep you stagnant and invisible forever. If you want to stand out and make a difference, continually finding ways to raise the bar is how you become the go-to referral for people in your community.

How to Move Past This Doubt

Start by acknowledging that your fear of not measuring up means you *want* to do things well. That's a good sign. Higher standards don't mean constant judgment. In the right culture, they mean better feedback, better tools, better coaching, and better outcomes for your clients.

Imagine two environments:

1. A place where nobody notices whether your contracts are tight, your marketing is strong, and your communication is clear.
2. A place where people care enough to say, "Hey, we can make this better. Let's do it together."

Which one is more likely to help you grow into the agent you want to be?

If you're worried about not being "good enough yet," here's a mindset shift that helped Jess reframe her doubt into belief: You don't join a higher-standard environment because you've arrived. You join it *because you want to arrive*.

> You don't join a higher-standard environment because you've arrived. You join it *because you want to arrive*.

You're not applying for a trophy. You're choosing better training partners.

And practically, you don't have to upgrade everything on day one. Growth usually looks like:

- Week 1: Tighten one process.
- Month 1: Upgrade one part of your marketing.
- Quarter 1: Work through one or two big skill gaps.

Step by step, your standards rise because you're in a place that expects and equips you to rise.

THE PERFECTIONISM TRAP

I see agents who mistake *excellence* for *perfection* all the time.

Perfection says, "I'll move when I have every answer."

Excellence says, "I'll move when I'm ready to grow."

Jess wrestled with this distinction. She'd scroll through other agents' feeds and compare their work to hers. "They've got better video gear and bigger budgets," she said during one of our meetings.

"They started somewhere too. Excellence is consistency, not cinematography," I'd remind her.

When she finally joined Raeco, she didn't wait for perfect conditions to start making the content she wanted to publish to build her brand. She brought her creativity with her, and within months she was making some of the most unique local videos in town that included home tours with humor, market updates with personality, and community features that felt genuine. She stopped chasing flawless and started creating connection.

The moment she gave herself permission to experiment, the numbers followed. Sellers called her because they recognized her face from social media, and her confidence grew because she was building on her own ideas, not borrowing scripts.

Perfectionism paralyzes, but progress compounds.

WHY GREAT AGENTS HESITATE

If you've already achieved success inside a Big Box system, you might be thinking, *Why rock the boat?*

That's the same thought that held Jess and so many other great agents in place for years. Jess wasn't afraid of failure, but she was afraid of losing momentum. The irony is that success creates the strongest comfort zones.

When everything looks fine on paper — when income is steady and your logo is recognizable — it's easy to confuse *familiar* with *secure*. But familiar isn't the same as fulfilling.

Driving home after our dinner at the Brick & Mortar Pub, the road between downtown and Lafayette was dark, and there were long stretches where the headlights of our car felt like the only light for miles. I thought about how many agents were driving the same metaphorical road — steady headlights, safe speed, but no real destination change.

Growth always asks for risk. The ones who say yes usually aren't the ones with the most to gain; they're the ones tired of wondering *what if*.

Jess's *what-if* turned into reality once she stopped treating change as loss. She realized switching brokerages wasn't starting over; it was taking everything she'd already built and setting it somewhere it could breathe.

Within her first year at Raeco, she'd expanded her business, added teammates, and built a personal brand that was unmistakably hers. Somewhere along the line, her comfort zone disappeared, and now she'll try anything that aligns with her standards and attracts attention. Today, she's the one other agents call for creative ideas.

Now, when I see her posting another creative campaign, I just think, *This is exactly what she was built for.* She found her stride by betting on herself, and you can have that same success too.

WHAT OVERCOMING DOUBT MEANS FOR YOU

If you're reading this and recognizing pieces of Jess's story in your own, take a deep breath, you're normal. Doubt doesn't mean you're weak; it means you care.

You've probably built a career that works. Clients trust you. Your phone rings. You've hit the level where people call you *established.* But somewhere between the closings and the commission checks, you sense there's supposed to be more — more ownership, more creativity, more connection.

That whisper is the beginning of change.

Here's what I've learned watching dozens of agents wrestle with internal doubts:

- **Fear thrives in isolation.** The longer you keep your questions to yourself, the bigger they get. Talk them out with someone who's walked the road before.
- **Clarity beats confidence.** You don't need to *feel* ready; you need to *see* clearly. Once you understand the difference between what you're giving up and what you're gaining, the decision makes itself.
- **Values make good compasses.** When you're torn, measure every option against what matters most: family, community, integrity, growth. The right choice usually honors all four.

I still think about my year-long conversation with Jess. It wasn't wasted time. Every hesitation she voiced helped me understand what holds agents back. Every doubt she shared gave me language to guide the next agent toward success.

Doubts are natural. They're the quiet questions that show up at midnight after a long day of showings.

Am I really capable of more? What if this is as good as it gets? What if I fail?

The truth is that every meaningful change comes with those questions. But doubt isn't the enemy, disconnection is. Once you reconnect with your purpose, doubt loses its grip.

Still, belief alone isn't enough. You also need a plan and a way to make the transition without blowing up what you've built.

Because once you've quieted the doubts, it's time to move from *What if?* to *Here's how.*

CHAPTER 8

TIME, MONEY, AND LIFE

"My favorite moment is when they tell me they're happy they made the move."

The Indianapolis 500 pit crew doesn't win the race, but they make winning possible. Watch them for a minute and focus on the blur of color, the hiss of the air gun, and the choreography that looks like chaos until you realize each person knows exactly where to be. There's no panic. No confusion. Every tool has a home. Every second has a purpose. For those seven seconds, the world goes silent except for the rhythm of the crew and the movements synced to muscle memory — precision and trust made tangible. Then, in a single breath, the car roars back to life and tears out of the pit, the echo of power swallowing the air left behind.

That's what Cassie built for Raeco.

Always willing to work alongside me, Cassie created our own version of a pit crew for agents making the switch to an independent brokerage that is fast, calm, and precise. She knew transitioning from a Big Box to a local brokerage shouldn't feel like tearing your business apart; it should feel like a well-rehearsed pit stop that gets you back in the race.

I like to say that if I'm the face of Raeco, Cassie is the rest of the body. She's the one making sure every moving piece works in rhythm so the team — and our agents — never lose stride.

Cassie would never call herself that, though. She'll tell you she's the behind-the-scenes engine. "I'm the one who takes all of Josh's ideas and visions and actually brings them to life," she says, usually while juggling QuickBooks tabs and a to-do list. "He's already moved on to the next idea by the time I'm finishing the last one."

She laughs when she says it, but she means it. Cassie doesn't crave the spotlight; she thrives in the quiet rhythm of making sure everything works exactly the way it should.

Most agents stay where they are longer than they should because moving seems hard. They picture chaos — paperwork everywhere, deals dropping, clients confused, spouses stressed — so they think, *I'll look at it after this quarter. After this listing. After I hit my cap.* And another year evaporates.

Transitioning brokerages doesn't have to be chaotic or risky. With the right systems, support, and mindset, it can be fast, stable, and surprisingly empowering. This chapter will show you the real cost of staying put, what a *good* transition should look and feel like, and how to find — or build — a pit crew of your own.

THE REAL COST OF STAYING PUT

Most agents stay where they are longer than they should because moving seems complicated and costly. But you don't really know that's another faulty belief until you sit down and look at the math to uncover the truth. The real cost of staying put isn't just the franchise fee on your check, it's:

- The lost income from better commission structures.
- The missed marketing opportunities you never get back.
- The community connections you could have deepened if your dollars stayed local.

Every month you wait, you're funding decisions you didn't make and supporting a brand that doesn't know your name.

Cassie likes to remind our agents, "When things get chaotic, it just makes it worse for everyone. The goal is to make it seamless and easy for everyone involved."

She's right. What feels safe often costs more than courage ever will.

And this isn't just about Raeco. If you're reading this and you don't live in Indiana, or maybe you're even thinking about starting your *own* local brokerage someday, the principle is the same: When you design (or look for) a transition that's calm, clear, and well-planned, you lower the emotional cost of change. You turn the big, scary jump into a series of small, doable steps.

Your job isn't to be brave enough to blow everything up. Your job is to be honest about what staying with a Big Box is costing you, and then insist on a plan that makes moving feel as safe as possible for you, your family, and your clients.

THE 12-POINT TRANSITION SYSTEM

When Cassie and I first started Raeco, onboarding was chaos. There were piles of paper on my desk, names were half-entered into systems, and there was the occasional contract that played hide-and-seek in the filing cabinet. But one day, Cassie stepped into my office, took one look at my desk, and said, "Nope. We're not doing this."

To bring order to the chaos, Cassie built what we now call our **12-Point Transition System** — not because there are literally twelve steps, but because it runs with the precision of a pit crew, each phase connecting seamlessly to the next. It's the rhythm that keeps everything moving.

Cassie laughs when people ask where it came from. "It started because I got tired of digging through Josh's piles of paper at tax time," she'll tell you. "Now everything from files to contracts and contact info has a place where it belongs, and we can see exactly where every person is in the onboarding process."

"The systems we have in place always have room for improvement," she admits, "but they keep the company running. If something happened and I couldn't make it in, I'm confident everything would keep moving. That's how you know your systems are working."

Once she got the initial operations under control, Cassie worked with a systems coach to refine the agent onboarding process, mapping out every action from the first call we have with someone to a full year after they switch their license to our brokerage. "You start with a full brain dump — getting every single step you can think of," she said. "Then you organize it into what needs to happen daily, weekly, monthly, or per agent. Once it's on paper, you can fix it. You can't refine chaos that's still in your head."

The system starts before an agent even signs paperwork. Cassie or I will walk them through what's coming and introduce them to Nelson, our marketing lead, so he can start gathering their info. That way, by the time ink hits paper, Nelson's already running and designing signage, updating email signatures, creating business cards, and drafting social posts. We give agents access to our Canva templates early so they can keep their listings active and their brand consistent.

Once marketing is in motion, Cassie's team tackles documentation. Contracts are simple and standardized, minimizing the friction of learning a new format. At the same time, we begin setting up technology — CRM, e-sign, email, and transaction software — and schedule meetings with our office staff to walk through the tools.

The administrative transition ties it all together to streamline direct deposits, license transfers, MLS access, compliance, and making sure every legal form is in the right place. Cassie oversees it all with what she calls "open communication."

"I tell every agent that we're available for any question, any time," she said. "The only bad question is the one you don't ask. We want this to feel easy, not intimidating."

And here's what makes Raeco's onboarding truly different — it doesn't end once the agent is fully onboarded. Cassie's system continues well beyond the first week. "We keep checking in at set intervals all through the first year," she explained. "It's about making sure things are still working the way they need to, that questions get answered, and that everyone stays on the same page as they grow."

That ongoing rhythm is why our transitions hold. It's not about speed; it's about stability. I call it Cassie's "pit crew" mindset: Everyone has their tool, everyone knows their timing, and no one leaves the line until the tires are tight.

And her golden rule? *If it's not on the calendar, it's not happening.* She laughs about it, but it's true. That rule keeps her sane — at home and at work.

Before she moves on to the next project, Cassie will often tell me, "The longer you wait, the harder it feels. Once you start, everything gets easier." It's that simple clarity that keeps Raeco grounded in progress instead of perfection.

How to Use The 12-Point Transition System

Even if you never step foot in one of our offices, this mindset is yours to borrow. If you're thinking about switching brokerages, here are a few questions to ask any potential new broker:

- **"What does your onboarding process look like, step by step?"**
  If a potential broker can't explain their process clearly, they probably don't have one.
- **"How do you protect my active deals during the transition?"**
  Listen for specifics about exit agreements and communication with clients and title companies, not just statements like, "We'll help with that."
- **"Who will be my point person during the transition?"**
  You shouldn't have to chase down half a dozen people to get the support you need. There should be one person you can text or call.
- **"What does support look like after the first week?"**
  Great transitions don't end with logins. They include 30, 60, and 90-day check-ins.

If you're dreaming about starting your own local brokerage one day, steal Cassie's playbook:

1. Brain dump every step of your ideal agent transition from an agent's first sign of interest to one year after they join your brokerage.
2. Sort each step of the process into categories like Before They Join, Week 1, Month 1, Quarter 1, Ongoing.
3. Turn these categories of activities into a checklist and calendar, not just good intentions.

You don't need to use the exact system we have at Raeco; you just need a plan that tells your agents (and your own nervous system), "We've thought this through. You're not jumping alone."

COMMON OBSTACLES THAT KEEP AGENTS FROM GOING LOCAL (AND HOW TO OVERCOME THEM)

I've heard every reason why agents delay a switch. Most of them sound practical, but, like the doubts we discussed in Chapter 7, they're really just fear in disguise. Let's name a few common fears agents have about transitioning from a Big Box to a local brokerage and talk about how to overcome them — no matter where you go.

Fear #1: I Don't Have Time for a Switch

This usually means, "My schedule already feels maxed out. I can't imagine adding one more thing." The reality is that a chaotic, unplanned transition *will* steal time, but a structured one gives it back.

How This Fear Shows Up:

- You push the decision off until "after this busy season," every season.
- You imagine weeks of disruption, confused clients, and late-night paperwork.

How to Beat This Fear:

- Ask potential brokerages for a sample transition timeline. If they don't have one, that's a red flag.
- Block time like you would for a big listing. Set aside two or three focused chunks of time over a couple of weeks to handle the move.
- Keep your active deals where they are until you and your new broker have a clear plan for transferring future business.

Cassie's take at Raeco is simple. She says, "You don't need more time. You need a checklist." We map transitions so precisely that an agent can move without missing a day of production. Marketing assets are prepped, files are transferred, and clients get their updates automatically.

Wherever you go, look for that same energy. Someone who says, **"We'll handle the heavy lifting so you can keep selling."**

Fear #2: The Paperwork Seems Overwhelming

You're already managing contracts, disclosures, and addenda. The idea of even more forms? No, thank you.

How This Fear Shows Up:

- You picture a dining room table buried in folders.
- You worry you'll miss a key step and get yourself (or your clients) in trouble.

How to Beat This Fear:

- Ask a potential brokerage directly, "Which parts of the transfer do you complete for me, and which parts are mine?"
- Ask for a written onboarding checklist so you can see what's coming and when.
- Break your own tasks into small, 20-minute chunks. Tack them onto your day instead of trying to do everything at once.

At Raeco, Cassie's response to the fear of overwhelming paperwork is simply to say, "That's what we're here for. We do as much of the work as we possibly can, so the transition is fast. We keep the agent selling while we do the switching."

You deserve that level of support, wherever you go.

Fear #3: My Spouse is Nervous About the Change

This one is huge — and valid. Your income affects more than just you.

How This Fear Shows Up:

- Your spouse asks, "Are you sure?" every time you bring it up.
- They want to see numbers, not just your enthusiasm.
- You feel caught between your own excitement and their caution.

How to Beat This Fear:

- Don't dodge your spouse's questions. Instead, bring them into the process.
- Request a meeting or Zoom call where your spouse can ask the new broker questions directly.
- Show them the math, including current splits and fees compared to your projected payment structure after the move, with conservative estimates.

Cassie smiles knowingly whenever an agent shares this fear. "That was me," she says. "I needed to see the plan, the numbers, and the backup plan when Josh wanted to make the switch to a local brokerage. Now I make sure every agent's spouse gets that same reassurance. The unknown feels a lot smaller when there's a checklist on the table."

Whether you join Raeco or not, include your spouse in the process. Let them see you're not leaping blindly, but that you're making a thoughtful, values-aligned move.

Fear #4: I Won't Be Able to Get Out of My Contract

Sometimes this is true. Often, it's just a story nobody's looked at closely enough to realize that there's always a way out.

How This Fear Shows Up:

- You remember signing something about committing to a year with your current brokerage, but haven't looked at the paperwork since.
- You assume leaving early means automatic disaster.

How to Beat This Fear:

- Pull your brokerage agreement and read it. Note dates, renewal terms, and penalties.
- Talk to a trusted broker or attorney if you're unsure what the language in your agreement means.
- Time your move with your renewal cycle or cap reset so you're not walking away from money you've already earned.

Most of the time, that "lock" is more of a knot that can be untied with the right timing. Cassie helps agents line up their departure with their renewal cycles so they don't lose a dime or a deal.

She says it best: "Everyone thinks switching is like jumping off a cliff. It's not. It's like stepping from one boat to another — you just need someone to hold it steady."

THE INVESTMENT VS. EXPENSE MINDSET

A franchise will call their fees "investments." But true investment means you get equity, ownership, and say in your future. Sending money up the chain isn't investment; it's rent.

Independent brokerages like Raeco flip that script. Your marketing spend becomes *your* brand. Your effort builds local recognition, not someone else's logo. And, done right, the systems turn overwhelm into ownership.

I like to think of it this way: Every dollar that stays local has compound interest. It funds the next sign order, the next agent event, and the next community sponsorship. You see the results where you live, not on a spreadsheet on a computer five states away.

Here's a quick test you can use to assess the ROI of your current situation:

1. Look at your last three closings.
2. Circle the dollars that left your paycheck in the form of company dollars, franchise fees, or required marketing.
3. Ask yourself, "**What did I actually get in return for that money — specifically?**"

If your answer is "brand awareness" and "access to tools," but you're the one doing 90 percent of the work anyway, you're not investing; you're renting.

Cassie always grounds me when I get too philosophical about it. "It's simple," she says. "If the work feels lighter and the money makes more sense, you made the right decision."

"If the work feels lighter and the money makes more sense, you made the right decision."

TIME, MONEY, AND LIFE

Transitions don't happen in a vacuum. They happen while you're juggling closings, kids' soccer games, and client calls. Life doesn't pause just because your business is changing.

Cassie gets that. She's lived it. "I've always been involved," she says, "but for years I was working full-time somewhere else while helping run the brokerage and raising three kids. Now I finally get to support the business, keep family at the top of the list, and help our agents do the same."

That's the real goal of a good transition system: **Your real life still works.**

You shouldn't have to ghost your clients, sacrifice every evening, or torch your family rhythm just to make a change.

If you're interviewing local brokerages — or sketching out your own future brokerage — listen for language like:

- "We'll plan around your existing contracts."
- "Here's how we protect your evenings and family time during the switch."
- "Let's map out a transition timeline that matches your life, not just our office hours."

I think most people make this kind of change a bigger deal in their heads than it actually is. Once we sit down and work through everything, they realize it's not scary. Clients choose you, not the logo on your sign. And when the dust settles, Cassie's favorite part is always the same: the quiet after the storm. The moment when an agent says they're happy they made the move.

At Raeco, we're not unique geniuses for figuring this out. We've just built systems based on the values you've already seen in earlier chapters: people over profit, rooted in local, built together, excellence, and a commitment to continue learning. Anyone who cares about their agents and their community can build similar systems in their town.

That's the beauty of a good system. It doesn't just move information. It moves people — from fear to confidence, from chaos to calm, from change to growth.

When the transition is handled well:

- You get your time back.
- The noise quiets down.

- You stop reacting and start creating.
- You finally have space to sell, to lead, and to live.

You deserve a move that feels like that, whether you join an existing local brokerage or build one of your own. So as you think about time, money, and life, here's the real question underneath all of this: **If the transition from Big Box to local brokerage didn't scare you, what kind of business would you actually choose?**

> If the transition from Big Box to local brokerage didn't scare you, what kind of business would you actually choose?

CHAPTER 9

WHY LOCAL AND NIMBLE WINS

"You don't need to fear the change ahead. You just need to choose the kind of company that's built for it."

Technology is rewriting the rules of real estate faster than ever. From AI-written listing descriptions to predictive lead scoring, what used to take hours now happens in seconds. It's a fascinating time to be in this business — if you know how to steer the tools instead of being steered by them.

Every week, there's a new app promising to automate one more piece of our work. Some agents are nervous about it. Others think it'll replace us entirely. The truth, as always, sits in the middle. AI can write your property remarks, but it can't walk through a house and feel the creak in the floorboards that tells a story. It can predict who might move next year, but it can't sit at a kitchen table and read the worry in a seller's eyes when they ask, "Will our house even sell right now?"

At Raeco, we've chosen to **embrace AI where it speeds us up** — drafting descriptions, summarizing reports, improving efficiency — but we always **humanize the output**. Every listing, every message, every marketing campaign still runs through the filter of local knowledge and personal connection.

The tools save us time, but the relationships earn us trust. That's the balance that separates strong agents from average ones.

The agents who thrive won't be the ones who try to out-code technology; they'll be the ones who use it to buy back time for what can't be automated, like conversations, relationships, and building trust.

> The tools save us time, but the relationships earn us trust. That's the balance that separates strong agents from average ones.

Real estate will always be a people-first business. Even as AI reshapes our workflow, the business still happens in kitchens, at closing tables, and in community events where people decide who they trust with their biggest financial decision. The algorithm can't replace the handshake.

Instead of worrying whether AI will take your job, this chapter will show you how to leverage new tools — and the local, nimble model — to *protect* your career, deepen your value, and future-proof your business, whether you stay where you are or decide to move. You'll see why staying local isn't just a preference; it's a long-term strategy for protecting your income, your relevance, and your career — no matter what the industry throws your way.

THE "ENEMY OF THE STATE" PRINCIPLE

If you've ever worked for a national brokerage, you've seen how decisions travel up the ladder before they ever come back down. The higher the ladder, the slower the movement. By the time a new policy, platform, or marketing change makes it to the agents, the market has already shifted again.

This is what I call the "enemy of the state" problem. Large brokerages are like aircraft carriers — massive, powerful, but painfully slow to turn. Local independent firms are speedboats. When the market bends, we can pivot in real time.

We've lived that advantage more than once. Late last summer, when listing views started dipping across every platform, we didn't wait for a quarterly report to tell us what to do. Nelson, our in-house marketing guru, pulled the numbers, spotted the trend, and called a quick huddle. Within a week, we'd shifted our strategy to feature short video walkthroughs on every listing. While bigger firms were still discussing budgets and brand guidelines, our new videos were already live and pulling triple the engagement.

That's what local ownership looks like. When the people who make decisions are the same ones who see the data, action happens fast — and the results speak for themselves.

Big Box firms can't do that. They're not built to do so because their first responsibility is to their shareholders. In publicly traded brokerages, the board's job is to protect **investor returns**, not to prioritize the agent's success or the client's outcome. It's not personal — it's structural. But it means that agents often find themselves caught between profit margins and best practices.

Local brokerages have a different heartbeat. We answer to our clients and our community, not to Wall

Street. That's what makes nimble, local firms like ours more human, more responsive, and, frankly, more fun to work in.

If you're at a big national firm right now, I'm not shaming your choice. My goal is to help you see the tradeoffs clearly.

In a large system, you may get access to tools but not the ability to change how they're used. In a nimble, local firm, you may have fewer layers separating you from the responsibility of decision-making but far more influence over how the business adapts.

The question isn't, "Is big bad?" The question is, "When the world shifts again — and it will — how quickly can your company shift with it, and how much say will you have in that process?"

If you're staying put for now, that's okay. You can still act like a speedboat instead of an aircraft carrier. Here's how:

- **Watch your own numbers.** Don't wait for corporate reports to tell you what's happening in your clients' lives.
- **Experiment on a small scale.** Test a new video format, a new follow-up flow, or a new community event inside whatever guidelines you have.
- **Pay attention to response times.** Track how long it takes your brokerage to respond when you raise an idea or see a pattern. That response time is a clue about your long-term fit.

And if you're considering moving to a local brokerage — or starting your own one day — this is the edge you're signing up for. The ability to see, decide, and act before the big ships even start to turn is what will give you a competitive advantage, no matter how much technology changes.

FUTURE-PROOFING YOUR CAREER

If the past few years have taught us anything, it's that the only constant is change. Interest rates bounce like a pinball, the Department of Justice and National Association of REALTORS® legal shifts make headlines every few months, and regulations tighten one week and relax the next. Agents who depend on slow-moving systems to interpret those changes will always be behind.

When rules shift or the economy tightens, local brokerages adapt faster because they don't need a national script. We can listen to what's happening in our communities and act immediately.

You see this adaptability in smaller ways every week. Every agent knows the panic of a last-minute inspection issue like a cracked step, a missing handrail, or something minor that can hold up a closing. Because we keep strong relationships with local contractors and tradespeople, we can make one call and have repairs handled the same day.

Those partnerships keep deals alive and dollars circulating right here at home. That's the advantage of being woven into the fabric of the community. Relationships move faster than bureaucracy. When you know the people behind the process — not just their email addresses — you can solve problems before bigger firms even know they exist.

> Relationships move faster than bureaucracy.

Local brokerages also create a kind of **community stability** that national companies can't. When you're rooted in a town, you don't ride the economy's wave; you help shape it. Your business dollars, sponsorships, and volunteer hours stay in the same zip codes where you sell homes. That's real economic insulation. It's one more reason nimble, community-connected firms thrive when bigger systems stall.

There's no silver bullet that will guarantee success in the future, but there *is* a clear pattern among agents who stay relevant. To be successful, you must stay curious, connected, and community driven.

Adopt new tech but don't worship it. Learn constantly but stay grounded in relationships. Invest in your community, because that's the only marketing that compounds forever. This matters whether you're at a Big Box today or already in a local brokerage. Future-proofing is about *what you do*, not just where you hang your license.

Here's what that looks like in practice:

1. Technology Adoption with a Human Focus

Use AI and new platforms to save time, but never to shortcut service.

- Let AI draft your listing remarks, then add the details only you know about the property, like the way the light hits the kitchen at 4:00 p.m. and the smell of lilacs in the backyard in May.
- Use automation for reminders and follow-ups but send the voice memo or personal video when it really counts.
- Batch your tech work so you can protect blocks of time for actual conversations.

If you're at a big brokerage that rolls out tools slowly, don't wait for permission. Many of the best tools are available to individual agents. Start small with one AI tool, one scheduling app, one better CRM habit. Keep asking, "Does this give me more time with my people, or less?"

If you're at a nimble local firm — or building one — bake this into your culture: Tech is here to *serve* relationships, not replace them. Every tool you add should answer, "How does this help us take better care of our clients and our agents?"

2. Community Investment as Strategy

Sponsor local teams, join the Chamber of Commerce, and show up where people gather. Those moments of connection and genuine care for the community create name recognition that no algorithm can buy. This engagement doesn't have to be expensive or flashy. Here are some ways you can invest in your community:

- Show up at school fundraisers, town parades, and community cleanups not just as "the realtor," but as a neighbor.
- Share local businesses on your social media and tag them so your reach becomes their reach, and vice versa.
- Host small, simple events like coffee at a local shop, a homebuyer Q&A at the library, or a client appreciation night at a local park.

If your current brokerage doesn't prioritize community, you still can. Your personal brand can be "local and present" even if your company feels distant. That brand equity will follow you wherever you go.

If you eventually move to a local brokerage, you'll bring that gravity with you. And if you start your own, you'll already have the habit of showing up where it matters.

3. Continuous Learning Culture

The agents who win are the ones who stay humble enough to learn. Every market shift brings new best practices, and those who see it as a chance to grow, not a threat to survive, will always stay ahead.
Here's how you make learning nonnegotiable:

- Block one hour a week for "career practice," and spend time reading, watching, or talking with someone who challenges you.
- Study your own deals. Assess what went right, what went sideways, and what you'll do differently next time.
- Steal good ideas from other industries. How do they wow people?

If you're in a Big Box with generic training, treat it as a starting point, not the ceiling. Seek out niche coaches, local masterminds, or small groups of agents who actually share what's working *now*, not just what's in the slide deck.

If you're in a local firm, push for a continuous-learning culture. Ask your broker, "How can we keep sharpening together?" Offer to share what you're learning. The more your whole office grows, the more valuable your brand becomes.

According to the **National Association of REALTORS®' 2025 Member Profile**, 55% of REALTORS® are now affiliated with an independent company.

affiliated with an independent company. More than half the industry has already realized that the local path isn't the risk — it's the advantage.

The independent movement isn't a rebellion against the old guard; it's a recalibration of what this business was meant to be in the first place: neighbors helping neighbors build better lives through real estate.

The future belongs to agents who can blend **cutting-edge tools** with **deep community roots and real human connection** — those who move fast without losing touch. You don't need to fear the change ahead. You just need to choose the kind of company that's built for it.

So, the real question to ask is whether you're in a place that will change *with* you or a place that will hold you back when you try?

CHAPTER 10

WHAT REALLY MATTERS

"If things ever go sideways over here, Raeco's my backup plan."

Remember that conference room from Chapter 1? The one inside the new state-of-the-art office built in an old newspaper factory with cinderblock walls and a concrete floor that echoed with every step? That's where I first told Cheryl — my managing broker, my boss, and my friend — that I was leaving the Big Box model for good.

I can still see her sitting across from me, calm but curious, the kind of leader who cared enough to ask the hard questions.

"You really think you can do this?" she asked.

"I don't know yet," I said. "But I'll figure it out."

She studied me for a moment, then smiled. "All right. Then tell me: What's your goal?"

"It'd be great if someday I had 10 agents," I said.

Cheryl nodded, a half-smile in her eyes. "You've always aimed high," she said. "If anyone can make it work, it's you."

She slid my resignation letter across the table, not as a dismissal but as a quiet show of belief. That meeting ended softly, without fanfare, but it became one of those moments you don't realize is shaping the next chapter of your life until much later.

After I left, Cheryl stayed at that same Big Box brokerage for a while. Eventually, she accepted an offer from another national brand in town — one with even more agents and even bigger numbers. It was, by every outside measure, a step up.

She did what good managers do: led meetings, coached agents, and kept things organized. And every now and then, we'd grab coffee or see each other at a local event, and she'd smile and say, "I'm proud of you, Josh. Raeco's looking good."

Then she'd add with a little laugh, "If things ever go sideways over here, Raeco's my backup plan."

For a while, things *were* fine. But over time, she started noticing changes in corporate leadership and the franchise owners themselves. Decisions that once balanced people and profit began to tilt hard toward the latter. Policies were justified in spreadsheets instead of conversations. Morale slipped.

She told me, "They're making choices that don't feel like the company I agreed to work for."

Cheryl's always been steady, fair, and guided by a clear sense of right and wrong. When the brokerage she worked for started prioritizing dollars over character, she began asking herself some tough questions about alignment, loyalty, and the kind of legacy she wanted to leave.

Her "this is enough" moment didn't come with drama. It came through quiet frustration, another meeting about revenue targets, and another decision that rewarded numbers over people.

She told me later, "It wasn't one big thing. It was the moment I realized that every decision was about dollars and none were about character. That's not who I am."

That week, she called and said, "Remember how I used to say Raeco was my backup plan?"

I laughed. "Yeah?"

She paused, then said, "I think it's time I stop calling it that."

When she walked into our Lafayette office to talk seriously, it felt like déjà vu — but with the roles reversed.

I leaned in for a hug. "Funny," I said, "we've been here before."

"Yeah," she smiled, "but this time I'm the one resigning."

We sat down and talked about what mattered most to her now: her community, culture, and being part of a brokerage that made decisions she could stand behind. She wanted to work where integrity wasn't a talking point; it was the operating system.

Before she left that day, she said, "I don't need perfect. I just need to know the people making the decisions care about more than just the bottom line."

A few weeks later, she joined Raeco.

WHAT REALLY MATTERS

When I think about Cheryl's journey and the dozens of other agents who've sat across from me having the same conversation, it always comes down to one thing: what really matters in your career.

Forget the slogans for a minute. Forget the recruiting flyers. This is the part where you zoom out and ask, "What do I actually want my work to add up to?"

Here are five truths you need to understand about building a career and a legacy you can be proud of. If you can see these clearly and make decisions with them in mind, you'll be able to take your next step with a lot more peace — and a lot less second-guessing.

1. Security Isn't Safety

Big brands love to promise safety. But real security doesn't come from someone else's logo; it comes from control. You know what's happening. You decide how the money's spent and who it supports. The agents who sleep best at night are the ones close enough to the steering wheel to make their own corrections.

2. Growth Without Alignment Isn't Growth

You can climb the wrong ladder quickly. I've seen agents produce at record levels while feeling completely disconnected from the people signing their checks. Growth that costs you your values is just drift, not true success.

3. Legacy Outlasts Volume

Your production plaque fades. Your reputation doesn't. Every deal adds or subtracts from how people remember you. Legacy is built in the schools your kids attend, the charities you sponsor, and the clients who still wave to you at the farmers market.

4. Balance Is Built, Not Granted

No brokerage can hand you balance. You design it, one decision at a time. Choose clients who respect your time.

Set boundaries that let you actually enjoy the life you're building. Balance is ambition combined with integrity.

5. Culture Eats Everything

You can't out-produce a culture that drains you. When you work around people who share your values, excellence becomes the default. When you don't, burnout does. Choose culture first; the rest follows.

That's what really matters. Not the trophies, not the franchise flag. What matters is whether your career funds a life — and a legacy — you're proud of.

THE COMPOUND EFFECT OF ALIGNED CHOICES

It's easy to assume legacy is always delivered in a press release or flashy awards. But in reality, legacy grows quietly through small, consistent choices.

Cheryl's first truth was choosing alignment. Then she started mentoring new agents, helping them onboard better than she ever had. Then she refined our systems by making tiny improvements that saved time and reduced stress across the board.

Those small decisions ripple out. One change becomes momentum, and momentum becomes culture.

In real estate, we celebrate the big numbers. But if you zoom out, the lasting success stories are written in the small, steady acts done well.

Someday, someone will tell *your* story. Sure, they'll mention your production, but they'll talk longer about your reputation, your relationships, and the impact you left in your community.

Ask yourself:

- What do I want my career to *stand for*?
- Who's better because I did this work here?
- When the signs come down, what remains?

Legacy isn't about staying comfortable. It's about staying true.

The good news is that you don't have to overhaul your entire life tomorrow to move toward the legacy you want. You just have to choose one next right step that aligns with who you're becoming, not just who you've been.

> What do I want my career to stand for?

THE FULL-CIRCLE MOMENT

A few months after Cheryl joined Raeco, we were locking up the office together after a late training. The office was quiet, lights low, and the hum of the refrigerator replaced the hum of those old fluorescent lights.

She glanced around the room that was full of the laughter, the chatter, and the energy of agents who actually loved what they were building just a few minutes ago and said, "Remember that meeting, back in the newspaper office?"

I nodded.

"You said you wanted 10 agents." She smiled. "You sold yourself short. You did that in year one."

We both laughed. Same town, different room, completely different feel. Back then, our meeting ended with a question mark. Now, it feels like an exclamation point — not because of the agent count, but because those agents represent people who chose alignment over autopilot, and local over distant.

Cheryl didn't just join a different company. She chose a different story to be part of. And you can, too.

If you're reading this and you've ever thought, *Maybe a local brokerage will be my backup plan,* consider this your invitation to rethink it.

You don't have to burn bridges to cross a better one. You don't have to abandon success to find significance. You just have to decide that your career — and your community — deserve the best version of you.

Because in the end, what really matters isn't how big your brand is. It's whether your work builds something that lasts.

CHAPTER 11

CLAIMING YOUR LOCAL ADVANTAGE

"Be Local on Purpose"

You've made it all the way here, and that tells me something about you. Not only are you curious, but you care about your craft, your community, and your future. Over the last 10 chapters, we've walked together from the noise of corporate limits to the quiet confidence of local excellence. You've seen how people like Becky, Grant, Jess, and Cheryl turned "maybe someday" into "I'm so glad I did."

So, what now?

This final chapter is about turning what you've learned into motion. It's about finding your clarity, putting roots into your community, and growing the kind of mindset that keeps you moving forward long after the last page closes.

You don't need more options; you just need one clear path.

THREE STEPS TO TRANSFORM YOUR CAREER

The framework I'm about to share is the same one Cassie and I used at our kitchen table when Raeco was just a dream and a notebook, and the same one I've walked through with agents who were ready to move from *fine* to *fulfilled*. This framework consistently snaps fuzzy ideas into clear direction, turns guilt and second-guessing into confident decisions, and connects agents' day-to-day work with the bigger life and legacy they actually want.

If you commit to walking through these three steps honestly, you'll come out the other side with a career plan that actually fits *you*, your values, your family, your community, and your future.

Step 1: The Career Clarity Exercise

When Cassie and I first started Raeco Realty, we didn't have a big roadmap or investors waiting in the wings. What we did have was a kitchen table, a notebook, and a list of what mattered.

On one side of a page of that notebook, we wrote *What We Want*. On the other, *What We Don't*. It sounds simple, but that list shaped everything we built.

Under *What We Want*, we wrote things like:

- Be recognized in our community.
- Build a company that means something when people see the name.
- Make sure that if it says *Raeco Realty* on the contract, everyone knows that person is respected, reliable, and the real deal.

Our tagline — *Reputation. Reliability. Results.* — came out of that exercise. It wasn't marketing fluff; it was the promise we wanted to keep to our agents, our clients, and our town.

Then came *What We Don't Want*. In this column, we wrote things like:

- To be a place that took just anyone with a pulse.
- To chase headcount.
- To compromise our values to grow faster.

That list kept us honest.

Now it's your turn. Grab a blank page and draw a line down the middle. Title one column *What I Want* and the other *What I Don't Want*.

Think three to 10 years ahead. Don't just list goals — list the life you want to live.

Ask yourself:

- What kind of financial stability do I want?
- What kind of lifestyle gives me energy instead of draining it?
- What kind of legacy do I want to leave behind in my community?

This isn't about what sounds good on paper. It's about what feels right in your gut.

Clarity beats chaos every time. Once you know what you truly want, every decision becomes easier. Everything from which brokerage you align with to how you spend your time each week will be rooted in this list.

Step 2: The Community Investment Plan

When we opened Raeco's doors on December 1, 2017, we didn't have a lot of money. We had heart, hustle, and a belief that if we showed up for our community, the community would show up for us.

Two months later, in February 2018, we met with the United Way of Greater Lafayette. Cassie already had a relationship with someone over there, Stephanie Patacsil, and we shared our dream to build something that mattered locally. We couldn't sponsor a ball field or host a gala, but we wanted to start small and start right.

So we made a simple commitment: For every closing, Raeco Realty would donate 25 dollars to the United Way of Greater Lafayette in our client's name. United Way sent each client a co-branded thank-you card with both our logos and a note saying a donation had been made on their behalf.

It was a small gesture, but it spoke volumes. Clients felt connected to something bigger, and our community began to associate Raeco with giving, not just selling.

That's what a community investment plan looks like in real life.

Now, it's your turn to build yours.

Identify two or three local organizations that align with your values, like a youth sports league, a food pantry, a veterans' group, or a neighborhood development project. The key isn't to make a splash, just be consistent.

Yes, you'll have to sign the checks, but the real commitment you're making is to show up. Attend the events. Volunteer your time. Offer your skills where they'll make a difference. Think about the gaps your talents can fill.

And when you spend money, spend it local. From sign printing to photography to closing gifts, use local vendors. It might cost a few extra dollars, but the return on those relationships is priceless. That's how you live what you preach.

Your work is the heartbeat of your town. When your business helps other local businesses thrive, you're building your career *and* community equity.

> Your work is the heartbeat of your town. When your business helps other local businesses thrive, you're building your career *and* community equity.

Step 3: Mindset Development

The biggest difference I've seen between agents who grow and agents who plateau is in their mindset. You can have the best systems, tech, and marketing on the planet, but if you stop learning, you start declining. The most successful agents I know invest in their own growth long before they need it.

With that in mind, here's my short list of books I'd hand any growth-minded agent:

- ***Profit First*** by Mike Michalowicz: This book is Cassie's favorite. It'll teach you how to build a business that serves your goals, not the other way around.
- ***Buy Back Your Time*** by Dan Martell: A must-read for anyone who's ever said, "I'm too busy."

- *Unreasonable Hospitality* by Will Guidara: A masterclass in making people feel valued.
- *Giftology* by John Ruhlin: A reminder that generosity is strategy, not charity.
- *Built to Last* by Jim Collins: How great organizations stay great by staying true to their core.
- *Raving Fans* by Ken Blanchard: A guide to creating clients who can't stop talking about you.

You don't have to devour them all at once. Just pick one and start. Set aside 15 minutes a day over your morning coffee, lunch break, or whatever works. Growth is a muscle. The more consistently you train it, the stronger it gets.

If you want to lead others, lead yourself first.

Mindset development also looks like:

- Seeking out mentors and peers who will tell you the truth.
- Being willing to try, fail, adjust, and try again.
- Choosing curiosity over cynicism when the market or the industry shifts.

You can't control every headline. But you can control how prepared you are to respond.

BECOME THE LOCAL LEGEND

By now, you probably see pieces of yourself in the stories throughout this book. The agents who thrive in a local, independent brokerage share a few core traits, and I call these people our **Local Legend Agents**.

Local Legend Agents:

- Value excellence and community impact.
- Want to make decisions, not just follow them.
- Believe in continuous learning and growth.
- Seek authentic relationships over transactions.

They're chasing impact over headlines. They don't want to be famous everywhere; they want to be *unmistakable somewhere*. If that sounds like you, you're already halfway there. You just need a place that matches your values, amplifies your strengths, and lets you make a difference right where you live.

If you've been reading this and thinking, *Maybe this is my next step,* this is your invitation to call or email me directly — no pressure, no pitch, just a conversation. Maybe you've got questions, maybe you've got comments, or maybe you've already started building something local and want to compare notes. Whatever it is, I'd love to hear from you.

This isn't about recruiting; it's about connection. It's about helping good agents find a place where their work actually fits their life.

Bring your goals. Bring your questions. Bring your "someday." Let's talk about what's possible, and maybe even what you've been told isn't.

You can call me at (765) 237-9351.

YOUR NEXT CHAPTER STARTS HERE

Your career is too important to leave to chance. You've worked too hard to settle for "fine." You deserve a brokerage that invests in your success as much as you do.

If there's one thing I hope stays with you long after this book closes, it's the belief that you don't have to wait for permission to build the career you want. You already have everything you need to start: clarity, community, and a mindset that believes growth is possible.

You've seen what happens when local beats corporate, when integrity beats size, and when people choose to stay rooted where they live.

Now it's your turn. Join the movement. Be local on purpose. Become your community's local advantage.

Josh Shives
Founder, Raeco Realty

A PERSONAL NOTE FROM JOSH

Whether this book sparked a big decision or simply gave you one useful idea you can take back into your business, I'm grateful you spent this time with me.

If something here helped you see your work, your community, or your career in a new light, would you take a moment to share that?

Your honest review helps more agents discover that there's another path to success built on community, personal values, and real connection. Every review keeps this message moving and helps the right people find it when they need it most.

Thank you for reading, reflecting, and believing that local still matters. Keep showing up where you live and work. That's how we all win.

ACKNOWLEDGEMENTS

This book wouldn't exist without the people who believe in the idea that *local still matters*.

To my wife, Cassie, the backbone of both our business and our family, you've challenged every idea that wasn't ready, steadied every late-night decision, and reminded me that the best things we build start at home. Thank you for believing in this vision long before the numbers proved it right, and for walking this path with me every step of the way. Raeco isn't just my story; it's ours. You are as much a part of this company as I am, and everything we've built carries your touch.

To our kids, Raelynn, Paisley, and Cash, you are the "why" behind everything we do. Your laughter fills our home, your names fill our hearts, and your future inspires every decision we make. I hope you always see what's possible when courage meets conviction and faith meets hard work.

To the incredible support system around us, our family, friends, and everyone who has stepped in to help when life and business got a little crazy, thank you. The old saying that it takes a village couldn't be more true. Entrepreneurship can be unpredictable, demanding, and at times a little chaotic, but having a circle of people willing to step in and lift us up has made all the difference.

To my Raeco family, every agent, staff member, and partner who has chosen to be part of this mission, thank you for believing that local business can be done differently. You've turned an idea into a living culture. The stories in this book may highlight a few of you by name, but every milestone, every client served, and every community event we've been part of reflects your hard work and heart. You are the proof that local still wins. I am *eternally grateful* for each of you — for your belief, your commitment, and your heart for the communities we serve.

To the mentors mentioned in this book, and the many others who have helped shape me along the way, your lessons in leadership, generosity, and grit have influenced not only how I lead, but how I live. You've taught me that true success isn't measured only by numbers, but by impact.

To Nicole Gebhardt and the entire Niche Press team, thank you for helping me take years of thoughts, experiences, and half-formed ideas and shape them into something clear and lasting. Your partnership made this book better than I imagined.

To the communities that have embraced Raeco Realty and become our partners, thank you for trusting us to show up, give back, and grow alongside you. You are the heartbeat of this mission and the reason local will always matter.

And finally, to the readers, especially the agents who picked up this book because something inside them knows there's a better way, this is for you. May you find the courage to build your own version of *The Local Advantage* and to keep doing business where it matters most: right here at home.

ABOUT THE AUTHOR

Josh Shives is the founder of Raeco Realty, an independent, locally owned brokerage headquartered in Lafayette, Indiana, with additional offices throughout the region.

After years of success inside a national brokerage, Josh realized that something critical was missing from his work: authentic connection. He saw talented agents working hard while distant decision-makers and franchise fees pulled money and influence away from the very communities they served. In 2017, he and his wife, Cassie, decided to do things differently. Together, they launched Raeco Realty with a simple but powerful mission to **be local on purpose.**

Under Josh's leadership, Raeco Realty has grown into one of Indiana's most respected independent brokerages, known for its values-driven culture, commitment to community, and belief that agents deserve both freedom and support. His people-over-profit philosophy and hands-on mentoring have helped dozens of agents find success on their own terms.

Before real estate, Josh built his career in hospitality management, where he learned the importance of service, standards, and teamwork — lessons that continue to shape the way he leads today.

Outside of work, Josh is most at home surrounded by the people and places he loves. He and his wife,

Cassie, are raising three amazing kids who keep life full and grounded. Together, they enjoy sharing meals with friends at Lafayette's local restaurants, spending long summer days boating on Lake Freeman, and unwinding around a bonfire with their close-knit circle of lifelong friends — lovingly known as *The Crew* — where laughter, reflection, new ideas, and bourbon always seem to flow.

CONNECT WITH JOSH:

Email: Book@JoshShives.com
Website: JoshShives.com | RaecoRealty.com
Phone: (765) 237-9351
Facebook: Facebook.com/Josh.Shives
LinkedIn: LinkedIn.com/in/JoshShivesRealtor

www.ingramcontent.com/pod-product-compliance
Lightning Source LLC
LaVergne TN
LVHW011951070526
838202LV00054B/4901